CONFESSIONS OF A DIVORCE ASSASSIN

What you really need to know about your case, your kids, and your lawyer

DAVID CRUM, ESQ.

Published by Legal Imprints Publishing Ltd

Crum, David
Confessions of a Divorce Assassin / David Crum

ISBN 978-0-9968107-0-8

PRINTED IN THE UNITED STATES OF AMERICA

First Edition

Dedications

There are a handful of people without whom this book would not have been possible. First, to Alexia Paul, my writing cohort and neurosis antidote. Thank you for your input and wonderful insights.

To Wayne Story and Mike LeMoine, my friends, colleagues, and part-time mentors. Thank you for helping me to shape this book and bring it into sharp focus.

And most importantly, to my one and only, beautiful and intelligent wife of twenty-one years, Melissa Crum. Thank you for walking with me through the dark years and finally bringing me into the light.

Legal Disclaimer

Hey everyone, sorry for all the legal mumbo jumbo, but I don't want anyone to get the wrong idea about this book or how it is to be used. So please read the following legal disclaimer closely:

The reader should use this book only as a general guide because it is not meant to be a substitute for local, legal advice from a lawyer where the reader lives. The author has made every effort to provide accurate and current information but many decisions in legal matters are based on unique circumstances. Also, laws vary from state to state and different attorneys will have different opinions about handling various issues. The views in this book are based on the author's experience practicing law and his extensive research in the area of divorce and family law. Nothing in this book is intended to create an attorney-client relationship between the author and the reader. The publisher, Legal Imprints Publishing Ltd. Co. and the author have tried to make this book as accurate and thorough as possible. Typographical and substantive mistakes may inadvertently exist. Legal Imprints Publishing Ltd. Co. and the author shall have no liability or responsibility to any person or entity with respect to any loss or damage, caused, or alleged to be caused, directly or indirectly, by the information contained in this book. **If you do not want to be bound by this disclaimer, you may request a full refund from your seller within ten days of purchase.**

That being said, good luck with your divorce and your new lives afterward.

Table of Contents

About The Author

David Crum is a celebrated author, speaker, entrepreneur, and divorce lawyer. After graduating with a law degree from the George Washington University Law School, David moved to New Mexico, where he started a divorce and family law practice at the age of twenty-six.

David is now the managing attorney of three prestigious divorce and family law firms that follow the principles outlined in his book:

New Mexico Legal Group

ww.NewMexicoLegalGroup.com

Nebraska Legal Group

www.NebraskaLegalGroup.com,

Colorado Legal Group

www.ColoradoLegalGroup.com.

He is an eternal student of the law and continues to strive to deliver the best services and experiences possible to his clients.

David and his wife Melissa are avid mountain climbers and travelers. They split their time between the breathtaking desertscapes of New Mexico and the emerald city of Seattle. They have one daughter who has flown the nest for the (greener?) pastures of New York City.

Introduction

A number of years ago, at the very height of my legal career, I decided to stop taking cases. While most of the people in my legal community thought this was crazy, I had profound reasons for this decision.

I was the managing attorney at a prominent divorce and family law firm, and business was booming. But I could not shake the feeling, one that I had for a long time, that there was a far better way for divorce lawyers to provide representation, and that the divorce process did not have to destroy families as a normal course of business. I knew I would have to step back so that our firm could re-focus on client based representation and alternatives to the normal divorce process.

More importantly, I also knew that real change was only going to come from the clients themselves. I discovered that it was informed, empowered, and refocused clients more than anyone, who could change the system. And, I needed time to figure out how to make that happen.

This book is an attempt to communicate the truth about the divorce process, your lawyer, and how you should really be looking at your case. Where appropriate, I have combined numerous cases to illustrate a point more effectively. I have, of course, changed all client names. And to my local colleagues, please do not look for yourself in these pages. All "opposing counsels" are amalgams of lawyers I have dealt with at some point throughout the state, and throughout the country, in nearly twenty years of divorce and family law practice.

For those of you who are contemplating divorce or who may already be in the midst of one, I hope you find wisdom here. As incredible as it may sound, I truly believe that you can come out the other side of your divorce a better person and a better parent. I wish you all the best in your cases and in your new lives afterwards.

David Crum

Part I

The
Dark
Years

Chapter 1

Sorry I Broke Your Family

WHEN OPPOSING COUNSEL walked into the courtroom with her client, I was surprised to feel my stomach drop. She was a mediocre attorney at best – law firm drone, pale and unoriginal – but this morning she struck me as supremely confident, cocky even. Our case was terrible, yes, but she had refused to even discuss a resolution. We briefly nodded as she began pulling folders from the shapeless bag at her feet. Later she would be sobbing alone in an empty conference room, but neither of us knew that now.

Roger whispered to me that he needed to "take a leak." Out of real need or simply to escape the presence of his soon-to-be ex-wife, I didn't know. It was a hundred degrees outside in the desert heat, but inside, with the air conditioning blasting, I was uncomfortably cold. Divorce court was always a strange scene: the hush of papers shuffling as two people who were once a team faced off as enemies.

Roger and Candice McNamara had been married for 15 years and had a five-year-old son named Elliot. They shared a spacious home in the East Mountains outside of Albuquerque, out of which Roger ran their vitamin supplement business. When things between them began to fall apart, they fell apart quickly. Allegations of abuse (him), drinking (her) had led us to this moment in a freezing courtroom where a judge would decide who would live in the marital home while the case was pending. In most divorce cases, the husband and wife work out who temporarily moves out before ever seeing the inside of a courtroom, but Roger and Candice had entered this ring punching from the first bell.

It was the kind of case that played to all of my strengths. At 27, I was the sole proprietor of my own law firm, just beginning to hire staff, and hungry for work. I was fresh from a Top 20 law school back East and a job with the U.S. Attorney's Office, and I had been trained to win at all costs. My growing reputation in town as the go-to guy for highly contentious divorce cases was not something I discouraged. Once hired, I would go to war if that was what the client wanted, and of course it was what they always wanted. I would

4

play it as smart and mean as he or she could stomach, with only one goal: to win.

Roger returned to the table just as we rose for the entrance of Judge Rodriguez. A quiet, older man, I could only guess at how this judge would lean. He was thoughtful, but also prone to scathing verbal takedowns of lawyers and clients alike. On the one hand, opposing counsel probably had the best case: it would be in young Elliot's best interest to stay with his mom in the family home. Mother-and-child arguments were often successful, especially with a family man like Judge Rodriguez. But I knew Rodriguez might also go for the financial provider angle. As the family business was run out of a home office and a supply room in the basement, I argued that Roger should remain there while Candice and Elliot went to live ... well, it never crossed my mind where they would end up.

With Judge Rodriguez it was best to keep it simple and deferential. I made my arguments quickly, answered his questions and sat down. Ten minutes, tops. Opposing counsel talked on and on, twice as long as my argument. She said things like, "Judge, it's *obvious*..." and, "You really have no other choice than to..." I saw Rodriquez glance at the clock twice. Opposing counsel was her own worst enemy sometimes.

It wasn't long before Judge Rodriguez returned from his deliberation to give the decision: Roger would stay; Candice and Elliot would move out. Technically, it could have gone either way, but I was still shocked by the decision. I turned to opposing counsel with what I hoped was a collegial shrug of the shoulders and was surprised to see her visibly shaken. Candice had not moved from her seat, frozen. The boy, Elliot, was waiting in the hallway with his grandmother. He was a dark-haired, skinny, shy kid and I knew he would be looking questioningly from face to face as his parents emerged from the courtroom. I stayed at counsel table with Roger until his wife and her attorney left the room.

"Listen, Roger," I said. "You know, even though the judge made a ruling, the parties can still enter their own agreement. So, let me know if you want me to change anything, or give them more time to move out or whatever"

"Oh, hell no. I want the bitch out of there tomorrow. Go tell her lawyer I want her out ASAP."

"Got it."

"You were *awesome,* by the way."

"Thanks."

I left the courtroom to find opposing counsel. It was late in the afternoon and the courthouse was unusually quiet. I peeked into an empty conference room and saw her sitting with her back to me, head in hands, staring at a legal pad. At first I thought she was thinking through some proposal for her client. But then I noticed her shoulders moving up and down and heard her quiet sobs. I had *never* seen a lawyer cry before, and I had already seen a number of lawyers go through some God-awful things in court.

"Hey, Deborah, are you okay?" I asked quietly from the doorway.

She turned, face splotched and puffy, and had difficulty getting the words out. "No, David, I'm not okay."

I was confused, but slightly elated. After all, this was war, and I had just made my enemy weep.

The Battle Continues

I wish I could say that the bitter beginning of the McNamara divorce was atypical. Or that Roger and Candice retreated to their respective corners and decided to proceed with dignity and mutual respect. Instead, Candice replaced poor Deborah with Alicia Stone, the only attorney in town who scared me. Alicia was smart and aggressive, a skinny but imposing brunette in a power suit. Even in those early days of my Albuquerque practice, she and I had squared off more than once. While she made me nervous, she also elicited my most brilliant and devious legal performances.

The tone was set, and retribution began almost immediately with Candice filing a restraining order against her husband, claiming threatening phone calls. Police reports began piling up, demanding my time and ever more of Roger's money. These criminal charges weren't particularly compelling – all were eventually dismissed – but they were filed by the prosecutors and certainly gave an overall impression of wrongdoing. Candice then continued to escalate matters by attempting to restrict Elliot's visitations with his father.

We threw a few grenades back immediately: a response and a motion to award Roger full custody in spite of Candice being Elliot's primary caregiver. The boy was quickly becoming the focus of this divorce, with both parties attempting to prove themselves the better parent by dismantling the other. Roger was a bully, but Candice was not without her own problems, as shown by numerous incriminating items Roger provided: a photo of Candice in a cocktail dress passed out in front of an open refrigerator door, food everywhere; a diary entry from the previous year he had secretly photocopied: "Feeling so low today with everything that's going on. Maybe need to talk to a professional ... AA?? I know I've been drinking too much. Sometimes I think Roger and Elliot would be better off without me."

Candice's love of confessional writing – and alcohol – was making my job easy. Wouldn't a boy like Elliot be better off with a strong father figure, the family earner, rather than a depressive alcoholic? Of course, Accusation Street ran both ways, and I knew Alicia had access to voicemails Roger had left on Candice's phone: "Candice, I swear to God I will destroy you" (ok,

I could argue this was non-threatening, he meant in the litigation). And, "Candice ... you are a f-ing whore and world class bitch (not much I could do with that).

At this point, Alicia and I crossed the invisible, unacknowledged line into assassin mode. There is often a point in a contentious divorce where the clients simply lose control of the process. Instead of a delicate dance untangling a shared life, they supercharge their lawyers into the very things they were trained to do: argue, contest, confuse, manipulate, win at all costs. Emotions running high can be contagious, with anger, aggression, and a desire to triumph passing from client to lawyer and back to client with imperceptible ease. Of course it wasn't personal – I had nothing against Candice *per se* – but I had a job to do, and I really didn't care what happened to Candice or her son. Candice and Roger had set two pit bulls against each other, and now they were powerless to stop the bloodshed. And they were each paying a hefty sum for the privilege.

At this point, two months into the McNamara divorce proceedings, Alicia requested a custody evaluation with a psychologist, an outside expert who could make a recommendation to the judge. This was a process that could last six to eight months, sometimes much longer, and involved interviews with all concerned parties, their friends and colleagues, as well as personality and drug testing. With this development, Alicia and I now had another person to lobby on behalf of our clients. We would present all incriminating/supporting documents to the psychologist in an arrangement that is fundamentally incongruous: the two people who are most invested in their respective clients winning custody are now deeply involved in influencing the "independent" custody expert.

Burning the City to the Ground

The brawl continued into the New Year: fights over alimony, the value of the house, the value of the vitamin business. Alicia and I hired dueling experts to weigh in on the value of the business, with the resulting figures vastly out of synch. Everything was contentious, all positions extreme, fixed, and opposite. There would be weeks of quiet followed by demands for discovery, piles of paperwork, time consuming depositions. I hired an additional paralegal just to help with the McNamara case.

Meanwhile, my attorney fees were soaring. At this point in my nascent career, Roger was by far my most lucrative client. At home, I had a wife in grad school, a two-year-old daughter, and a giant student loan. I would work every day until 10 p.m., usually coming home after my daughter was asleep. I was a machine, hatching secret plans and legal strategies in dozens of divorce cases, and the McNamara case was getting my most vicious attention.

Within all this madness, a trial date was set for October. And, against my advice, Roger got himself a girlfriend who looked amazingly like Candice, only ten years younger. As soon as I heard, I wondered what this news would elicit from his wife. I knew it would be ugly and it was. Candice's lawyer hired a private investigator to trail Roger, as well as set up a hidden camera that pointed right at Roger's front door. The guy was good. The thick manila envelope that came to my office via messenger was a bombshell, containing videos showing Roger, his girlfriend, and Elliot entering the house in the evening, and Roger leaving alone in the mornings, sometimes not returning until evening – meaning Roger wasn't really using the home office and was leaving Elliot alone during the days with his girlfriend.

Candice and Alicia had built a convincing case that Roger was leaving Elliot in the girlfriend's care for the majority of the time. If she could persuade the judge to agree that Roger was not actually acting as the primary caregiver, it could go far in throwing custody in her favor. And the stakes were now higher than ever for who got to keep Elliot: both Candice and Roger were itching to leave Albuquerque. Neither had any family ties here, so Candice wanted to go back east while Roger had his sights set on California.

With October looming, I worked late into the evenings preparing for the five-day trial that was now sitting on Judge Rodriguez's docket. Most divorce

11

cases don't ever go to trial – judges hate them because they are expensive, time consuming, and usually extremely boring. But there would be no settlement agreement for the McNamaras, no mediators, no last minute reconciliation. There was just too much damage done and we were all too far gone.

Preparing this case was a huge undertaking, and when I took the time to analyze it from the other side, it was hard to avoid the conclusion that while Candice was certainly not a great parent, Elliot would probably be better off with her than with Roger. But you can't think about those things, not with a trial coming and your client having already spent a hundred grand in legal fees.

Then a lucky break: I was able to get the private investigator's evidence excluded as it was disclosed too close to our trial date. Without knowing what was in the videos, Judge Rodriguez agreed with me that such a late disclosure was prejudicial to our case. I thought Alicia would have a stroke.

Even then, walking into the courthouse on day one of the trial, all my confidence was a lie. Candice's family had flown in for the trial, and they were all lined up in the hallway as I made my way to the courtroom. Alicia was speaking with Candice's gray-permed mother and a man I didn't recognize. I fought the rising panic that Alicia had something up her sleeve I had not anticipated. Nearly everyone shot me a nasty look as I walked by.

When the trial started, an event at which Elliot was mercifully absent, Alicia drew first blood. Without a private settlement, our clients' flaws were now publicly on display, the light harsh and unforgiving. Roger, hulking in his best suit, took the stand first as Alicia paced the floor in high heels that sounded like little machine guns. Clack clack clack: "Mr. McNamara, upon first hearing your wife's plan to leave you, you grabbed her arm so hard that you left bruising, correct?"

"Yes, I did grab her arm."

"Hard enough to cause bruising, yes?"

"... uhm ... yes, I guess there was a bruise.

"There were several bruises, yes?"

"Yes, that's right."

Clack clack clack: "And, is this your voice leaving the following message on your wife's voicemail?" Static played over the speakers and then came Roger's clear baritone: "Well, well, well...you f*ing did it this time. I'm going to come over there one night and you'll be sorry."

"Yes ... but I didn't really mean anything by it."

After several hours of this torture, it was my turn. Candice was put-together and calm as she took the stand. I began, friendly and non-confrontational: "Have you ever hired a babysitter for Elliot, Candice?"

"Sure."

"And, as a parent, there are certain people you would never leave your child with, right?"

"Yes."

"Like someone who abuses alcohol."

"Right."

"Like someone who is suicidal."

"That's right."

"Someone like that, you wouldn't leave your kid alone with them for even a minute because it would be far too dangerous, correct?"

"That's correct."

Less friendly now: "And the truth is, you are all of those things, aren't you, Candice?"

And after each denial I pulled another document from the file to impeach Candice's testimony: the photos, the journal entries, medical records, a suicide note she had hidden in her closet. Candice was finally speechless and quivering when the judge allowed her off the stand. She sat back down next to Alicia, and even Alicia, who never showed emotion, looked like she'd been punched in the stomach.

The psychologist then took the stand, recommending that Roger have primary physical custody of Elliot if he agreed to attend anger management therapy, and that Roger could take Elliot to California.

Alicia was good, but I was better, and we prevailed on almost every issue. Roger would be moving to California with Elliot and paying Candice the alimony we suggested to the judge, which was far, far lower than what Alicia was requesting. The boy would be with his mom most holidays and a few weeks in the summer. We had won the war but the city had been burned to the ground. Still, my client was happy, so I was happy.

Aftermath

Three years later, with a swelling caseload, the McNamara case was a distant memory. Pushing through a happy hour crowd, martini in hand, I ran into Alicia.

"Remember that crazy McNamara case we had together?" she asked.

"Of course. What a mess."

"Have you talked to Roger since it was over?" "Nope."

"You're going to love this then. Candice called me a couple of weeks ago just to let me know that she and Roger were both living in Glendale."

"You've got to be kidding me."

As it turned out, after everything had blown away – the character attacks, threats of violence, anger, sadness, and over $250,000 in legal fees – Roger and Candice had worked it out on their own, without our "help." Roger was paying three times the alimony required by the judge; Candice attended AA meetings regularly; and Elliot enjoyed two parents who weren't at war.

Had they known what they were getting into when those words: "I want a divorce," were first shot across the bow, would they have done things differently? What if someone had been there to say, "Wait a minute! Don't call that divorce lawyer just yet. Even though it will still hurt, there's a way to do this without engaging in a war you will lose, even if you win."

People choosing to dissolve their marriages are often in an impossible position, a position in which it can be difficult to think clearly and make good decisions about the future. And unfortunately, a consultation with a divorce lawyer can be the very worst place to start the process.

When I was a young lawyer, I practiced law exactly how I was taught – to "win," no matter the emotional cost. It's not that lawyers or their clients are bad people. It's just that today's divorce processes and the roles that the participants play are not designed to achieve an outcome that reflects a family's real-world needs. Every divorce is unique, thus the process of separation should be individualized, tailored to fit each family. But, unlike a professional mediator, most divorce attorneys are not trained to take a holistic, customized approach. They are working from a template, a rote battle plan designed to get their client the biggest piece of the pie, whatever the emotional cost. Adding to the confusion, the parties themselves are too often distracted by anger and revenge to keep their eyes on the prize: what they *really need.*

Divorcing parties must be able to take control of their cases and understand the options that are available to them; and learning how to do that should start *long* before they ever talk to a lawyer. That is the purpose of this book: to encourage those who are considering divorce to take ownership of the process rather than surrendering their power to seeming "experts". The customary path to separation in this country is a machine that takes an already troubled family and chews it to bits. But it doesn't have to be this way. There is a more peaceable solution that can help those who choose to divorce get through a difficult time in the least destructive manner possible.

Chapter 2

The Assassin's Training Ground

A LAWYER IS NEVER entirely comfortable with a friendly divorce, anymore than a good mortician wants to finish his job and then have the patient sit up on the table.

– Jean Kerr

Let's take a step back. Why is divorce in this country such a catastrophe? When asked about the arduous process of separation, most people are quick to point a finger at the cold, pinstriped heart of the divorce lawyer. And why wouldn't they? Who else is to blame for ratcheting up the conflict, turning your kid into a negotiating chip, and funneling your hard-earned money directly into his bank account? A divorce lawyer isn't viewed in the same light as the noble defense attorney, the righteous prosecutor, or even the ambitious corporate counsel. He is rarely seen in a hero's role.

But divorce attorneys are not born; they are made. They are young men and women who, for whatever reason, chose to attend law school. And sure, there they learn the nuts and bolts of the law, but on a more fundamental level, law students are taught a specific way to think. Each spring, a new crop of young attorneys throws their mortarboards in the air and heads off into the world trained to argue beyond all reason, deflect blame, confuse the issues, cast doubt, gain leverage, to find a way to win, always to win. This is the very skill set that is then brought into the divorce process. Overall, it is such a mismatch between what a family really needs and what the lawyer has been taught to provide, that the results can be truly disastrous.

Thus, once you've set up that first meeting with a divorce lawyer, it's very likely that you've already lost. Not because divorce attorneys are evil people, but because, understandably, most are bound to use the skills with which they have been trained.

Assassins are Made, Not Born

I first stepped foot on the urban, non-campus of George Washington University Law School in 1991. No grass green quads and ivy-strewn gothic here: classes and dorms are located in downtown Washington, D.C., abutting office buildings and restaurants and police stations. But what it lacked in collegial ambiance the school made up for in sheer east coast ambition and a solid gold list of well-heeled alumni. Raised in a conservative Midwestern city by middle-class parents who were disdainful of lawyers ("a dime a dozen"), GW was Phase II of my grand escape after four years spent earning my undergraduate degree in Boston.

By year two, I was confident in my role as law student, but still I submitted my class schedule with trepidation. Against my better judgment, I had signed up for the seemingly innocuous class "Negotiations," the class reputed as a must-take for anyone who was serious about becoming a great lawyer. But I knew better. I knew this class would take me *way* out of my comfort zone. Growing up middle class, you don't talk about money, or making deals. The price is the price. If you can't afford it, it's just embarrassing. But here, we would be expected to negotiate *everything*.

One week in, we were paired up for our first graded exercise. Each student faced off against his or her partner, attempting to negotiate the best deal possible based upon a fact pattern provided by the professor. The kid sitting across from me was thin and pale and looked barely out of high school. I relaxed. How bad could this be? He steepled his fingers like some child tycoon and began, "What are you thinking?"

"Oh ... I was just thinking we should try to reach something that's a win-win," I replied.

"Like a compromise agreement, you mean?"

"Exactly."

"That sounds great," the kid said. "I was really worried this was going to be so awkward."

And from there he proceeded to let me know what he needed, what was most important, what he didn't care about, and what he could give me in exchange for what I needed. And in return I shared the same things with him. We finished and the class was only half over.

"Pretty easy, eh?" he said, folding his hands behind his head and leaning back.

"Yep."

The following week we returned to class, anticipating the results of our negotiation exercise. I arrived barely on time, and as the heavy door slammed shut every eyeball in the stadium-seated room was suddenly trained on me. I spotted my partner down front. He turned away quickly to face the blackboard, where a list of student names and scores were printed in neatly arranged columns. There was also a key depicting how each issue correlated with the points awarded by the professor. I descended the oddly spaced stairs, and my face flamed as the blur of names cleared: at the top of the long list was my partner's name; at the very bottom was mine – and next to it a zero.

The kid had really played me, affecting nonchalance about key items while oh-so-generously giving away the ones that didn't matter in the least. After the interminable class ended, I caught up with him in the hallway. "So, what, was that all bullshit?"

"Oh, come on, man. You heard the professor: it is what it is."

Indeed. It is what it is: a system in which there is no reward for reaching common ground or finding creative solutions so that everyone walks away with something. No, the students who clawed, cried, pouted, intimidated, or outright lied to get the *most* received the best grade. Law school was an island where all the fundamental values I had learned as a child – courtesy, honesty, a spirit of give-and-take – were suddenly of no value at all.

The many A-list speakers the university brought in to impart their wisdom on our impressionable souls only enhanced this worldview. People like Michael Jordan's agent, who boasted of his extreme negotiation tactics: hammering out Jordan's salary, he recalled his Soviet-style demand on the NBA, "I know none of you are going to think this is reasonable, but before this is over you'll be begging me to accept this number." Or, the lawyers who won Lorena Bobbitt's acquittal: she didn't do it; even if she did do it, she didn't do it on purpose; even if she did do it on purpose, she had a legal defense for doing it; and on and on until the issue was a confusing muddle of intent and justification.

And then there was the former U.S. Attorney who basked in a story from his days in private practice. He bragged about how he had drawn a plaintiff's lawyer into the issue of on which side of the road an accident had occurred, even though it had zero relevance on the issue of liability. And when the plaintiff's lawyer finally realized what was happening and explained to the jury that it didn't matter on which side of the road the accident occurred, the U.S. Attorney turned the table, "Then why in the hell did he argue about it for a week?" The jury decided to award zero dollars to the victims in the case.

These experts glamorized a process that, from an outsider's perspective, seems absurd. We were taught never to ask a question to which we did not already know the answer. We were taught to make trials not about the actual issues, but about issues we could win. We were taught to find a way around even the most obvious facts, to confuse, cast doubt, and deflect blame. Three years steeped in this environment trained us to accept this win-at-all-costs worldview as a new way of life. Conflict was no longer an uncomfortable part of life; it was what we thrived on.

Why the Training Ground Matters

What does all this training mean for you? How does it play out in the real world of divorce, where emotions run high and skills such as empathy and needs-based negotiation are key? The fact is, family law is not a core course taught at most law schools. It can be chosen as an elective, but this subject is not in high demand among 23-year-olds with their eyes on more lucrative or noble-sounding futures. Your lawyer may very well have graduated without ever taking such a class. So where did she acquire the skills she now needs to be a great, compassionate divorce attorney? All too often, she simply didn't. She will rely on the adversarial model she learned in school and you will pay the price.

Not many students attend law school to become divorce lawyers. So, why can you go online and see page after page of local attorneys competing for these cases? Here is how a divorce lawyer is often built: let's imagine Kevin, out of law school for three years at a low-paying job at the District Attorney's office. Kevin is still saddled with a glacial hunk of student loans, so he decides to open his own practice and make a real go of it. At Kevin & Associates, he takes on whatever cases he can get: criminal, family law, personal injury. Does he take continuing education courses to expand his skills in the area of divorce and family law? Probably not – these classes are expensive and he's got a business to run, so he takes only the minimal requirements to keep his license. He knows the basics and has his diploma framed and hung. It is enough. Kevin is charming, can talk the smooth talk and shake hands like a pro. He approaches whatever case he's working the same way, knows his basic strategy, and tries as hard as he can to make the case as profitable as he can.

When a divorce client walks through the door, Kevin knows exactly what that person wants to hear, so the consultation is all about how Kevin will fight for the client, get the best result possible, destroy the other side if that is what's desired. Kevin is far from a family law specialist, and has no idea what it takes to preserve a healthy family *after* divorce, so it's all hammer and no nuance. Things like 50/50 custody all the way if it's the dad, and hardly any visitation if he's representing mom. Maximum spousal support if he represents the stay-at-home parent, or hardly any support if he represents the breadwinner. Never mind that 50/50 custody is often a nightmare for a kid who feels she's perpetually living out of a backpack. Never mind that taking extreme positions on spousal support totally misses the financial realities of these broken families

What you hear from many lawyers is that they hate these cases. They have no control over them, can't make money, can't deal with their clients' emotional issues. Divorce is different from other areas of the law because it involves so many emotional pressure points:

relationships, kids, finances, the future, emotional problems. Instead of the black and white worldview taught at law school, divorce is a palate of murky grays.

There are almost one million lawyers practicing in the U.S. today [1] No matter what type of law they specialize in, most were trained in the same kill or be killed logic. But great lawyers – those who practice family law especially – live in the real world, not the world of law school. In the real world, emotional landscapes matter, and compromise and cooperation can make an extremely difficult circumstance at least tolerable, and – in some cases – a divorce can completely transform people in a positive way.

Out on My Own

By the end of law school I had been thrust into the furnace, melted down, reshaped, and allowed to harden. And by then I thoroughly hated the idea of being a lawyer. My classmates were shooting stars fueled by ambition and the heavy weight of debt. They found jobs in D.C. or were bound for New York, Chicago, or San Francisco. Turning my back on all that shiny potential, my girlfriend Melissa and I headed to the Southwest for open skies and brighter

---

[1] http://www.cnbc.com/id/100569350

days: the serene desert-scape of New Mexico and a more mellow life … or so I thought.

Arriving in Albuquerque with no money, significant credit card debt, and stifling student loans, my options were limited. Sure, I had my law degree, but I was looking at one of the worst legal job markets in recent history. So I used my considerable powers of persuasion to land a job as a truck driver for a delivery company. I spent that first hot desert summer studying for the New Mexico Bar examination and delivering lost luggage to rich people in Corrales.

After I passed the bar, and maybe after watching *A Few Good Men* one too many times, I decided to skip over the "real" job part where I could have learned how to actually practice law, and opened my own firm.

Crum & Associates was born in a small part of a large two-story building owned by a prestigious employment lawyer. While I struggled to build my client base, I pounced on my unsuspecting landlord with a thousand questions about the practice of law. I honestly would not have made it through that first year without his patient answers to my questions.

Like many solo practitioners, I started taking on divorce cases (among other things) because of cash flow needs. At the same time, I was handling criminal cases, filing bankruptcies, taking on employment cases, and spreading myself as thin as humanly possible. But then a funny thing happened: it became clear that I had quite possibly been put on this planet simply to be a divorce lawyer. There was something in my makeup that allowed me to really communicate with the most pathetic or most successful client who walked into my office. I was loved by the downtrodden (whose parents paid my bills) as well as the rich (who paid their own bills). And I loved the potential ambiguity of these cases, the adversarial nature of the process, the emotional highs and lows and extreme unpredictability. I loved to fight, didn't mind the mess, listened to the most depraved stories, and sympathized with the saddest characters. It wasn't long before other lawyers in the community began referring me the complicated divorce cases they were more than happy to dodge. I hired a paralegal and began taking legal seminars in every area that related to divorce.

Melissa and I were married, and while she went to grad school and took care of our infant daughter, I painstakingly taught myself how to run a law firm. And as more and more cases came my way, I honed my assassination skills to a fine point. I became the guy who pulled no punches, the lawyer you *did not* want your ex to hire.

What I noticed during those first few years in practice was that a large number of my colleagues – the "Kevins" who took on divorce cases to pay the bills – were doing a true disservice to their clients. They didn't have systems or staff set up to handle their cases properly. They had no control over their clients. Most were just waiting to do something else, or for a big personal injury case to come in. Law school had not prepared them; they had no interest in family law, and they did nothing to develop their skills or expertise in this specialty. Even worse, the big firms who specialized in divorce and family law seemed to run a "check-the-box" practice that maximized conflict, as well as their fees. In one particular case, when the court required the firms to provide their total attorney fees to the court, my opposing counsel's fees were more than twice what I had charged ... and I had undoubtedly gotten the better deal for my client.

A Slow Rise to Stardom

"David, your three o'clock is on line one!" This was Greg, my brother-in-law/legal assistant/recent college graduate, who had moved to New Mexico to help with the practice. Greg would eventually become a lawyer himself, but when he worked for me, he had a near genius ability to sign up new clients. It didn't hurt that he also looked like a movie star who had just relocated from LA.

Kathy, on line one, was calling from Idaho. She had divorced her husband Rick two years earlier and had taken their child to Idaho with Rick's consent. Now, after a routine summer visit, Rick had failed to return the child. Rick claimed that mom was using drugs and that it was best for the child to stay with him. And then Rick just disappeared.

In the screening call, Greg had determined that Kathy had no money, but that her parents were willing and able to spend whatever was necessary to get their grandchild back. So, on this first call I was working with a $25,000 retainer.

This case was not a problem at all. Within forty-eight hours my investigator had found where Rick was living: Estancia, New Mexico. And by the next day I had filed an Emergency Motion for Return of Child with the Estancia District Court.

Greg and I arrived in Estancia early for the motion hearing, wondering if Rick would actually appear. I drank coffee while Greg organized our exhibits. And then here came Rick, pushing hurriedly through the courtroom doors, court papers in a heaping mess as he plopped down at the opposing counsel table and shot a challenging look in my direction. Kathy sat between us, avoiding eye contact with her ex.

"Well, I see Kathy has a hired gun. Real nice. I guess you don't care about what happens to our son, huh?"

"Kathy's made it pretty clear to me that your son shouldn't be with you at all," I said.

"Well, I think you're a total a-hole." Greg started to rise from his seat, but I put a hand on his shoulder. "A total a-hole is what I think. And I'm going to let the judge know what's really going on here."

"That's good," I said. "We can both let the judge know what's going on and then he can make his decision."

Not long after the judge took the bench, he ordered the child returned to his mother immediately and before I knew exactly what was happening, I was driving into the desert with Kathy by my side and Greg in the back seat. Estancia proper gave way to rocky scrabble as we rode behind a long line of police cruisers with cops ready to smack Rick down at the first sign of resistance. At the end of a long dirt road there was a single trailer home, with Rick's girlfriend standing outside scowling, the child in her arms.

In a small town like Estancia this was big news, so as Kathy and I ran to get her son, every cop in town must have been on the scene.

"Honey, this is David, the lawyer who *brought you back to me*." That's what every law enforcement officer in Estancia heard as she took the kid back into her arms. And cops, God bless them, they are the worst gossips in the world. So this little story spread like wildfire all the way back up to Albuquerque, to all their cop buddies, prosecutors, defense lawyers, and judges. And suddenly everyone was sending me every type of family law case that came his way. My reputation as the go-to guy for high conflict divorce cases was officially solidified.

The Takeaway

So what does all of this mean to you and your case? What are your options as you enter the brittle, often painful experience of divorce? Thanks to how lawyers are trained, you can either hire a half-assed divorce attorney (Kevin) or one who is super-aggressive (the old me) or a high-rise, high reputation, by-the-numbers divorce firm. But none of these options is going to help you survive your divorce with the least amount of destruction possible. None will help you get what you really need.

Chapter 3

Lessons from a Very Rich Woman

"**Y**OU MISSED IT."

"I missed it." I didn't know what my wife Melissa was referring to, but I did know better than to argue. I had been missing a lot recently – dinners, date nights, and now it dawned on me: Cali's soccer game to which I'd absolutely sworn I would go. But there had been no way to leave the office for her 6:30 pm game. There was simply no end to the briefs, meetings, staff issues, court dates, and filings. I could spend all day and night in my office and never be as prepared as I would like to be.

"She finally scored, David."

"Aww... shit. I'm sorry, sweetheart."

"Don't be sorry to *me.*"

According to Hollywood, lawyers are verbal geniuses, peacocking around courtrooms throughout the court system, trying to outwit one another. In movie trials, the zingers come fast, off the cuff, and the attorney to root for operates on people skills and gut instinct. She's *just that good.* The sad, unsexy truth of practicing law, however, is that the lawyer who is *most prepared* usually achieves the best result.

In a divorce case, this means preparing for everything that can, and will, go wrong, and anticipating all arguments that opposing counsel will throw your way. Within the often-unpredictable world of divorce, knowledge is certainly power, and a little organization goes a long way. As ever higher-conflict divorce cases showed up at my door, these two truisms forced me to take action. Divorce can be a messy business and sternly resists being put into a neat little box. The only way I knew to wrangle the beast was to create a number of efficiency systems that provided a framework within which to operate. I made checklists for everything: asset/debt calculations, discovery requests, custody petitions and counter-petitions, settlement agreement worksheets, parenting plan checklists. And on top of this I piled reams of sample language, legal clauses, releases, acknowledgements, stipulations, escape hatches ... the list went on and on. There are hundreds of different items that a lawyer should consider when handling a complete divorce case. Perhaps a small portion of these items actually applies to a specific divorce, but due diligence demands checking each one off the list. I also engaged in a comprehensive overhaul of my office and staff operations, developing a series of procedures that included telephone blocks, work blocks, client binders, comprehensive client screening, and delegation to the least level of competence, among others.

These systems served to limit oversights and mistakes, kept the cases moving forward, and whittled down the myriad issues at hand to the items my clients *actually* needed. Within an hour of meeting a new client, I had a nearly full view of everything I needed and didn't need to do. But this was more than simply an exercise in uber-efficiency. As my practice and reputation grew, these systems gave me the sense of control I craved. People were falling apart all around me – in my office, on the phone: crying, yelling, threatening, stone cold with anger. And I could simply retreat to my excel spreadsheets. What do you need to know? It's all here in black and white; let's plug in the numbers and get you the *best* result possible. Despite their emotional turmoil, my clients could flow through these systems with clear direction and organization toward a predetermined goal.

This process gave me an enormous advantage over opposing counsel, many of whom were sloppy at best, incompetent at worst. After all, it is easier to employ the blunt tools of our trade: push a button, email an 85-page discovery request, and bill five hours for the effort. Let the other guy drown in paperwork. Never mind that half of the information requested has nothing to do with the realities of the case at hand. This rote handling of divorce cases has two unfortunate consequences: the chaos of too much unorganized information means that key items often go missing, and unnecessary paperwork and court appearances increase costs exponentially. You get less bang for your buck.

The View from the Top

By 2002, Crum & Associates had blossomed from a guy with a law degree who loved a good fight to an established practice. I had my staff in place, my systems in place, and was at the height of my litigation superpowers. Into this scene walked Jackie, a local girl who had married – and was now divorcing – Derrick, her high school sweetheart. Jackie was referred to me by one of my classmates from GW Law. Jackie had a high profile consulting job in D.C. and was the primary breadwinner in her family. Though there was little rancor between Jackie and Derrick, the case was complicated. They had two young children. She had some vested and unvested stock options; there were separate property issues, and investment accounts to disperse. And, given their income disparity, it looked like she might owe a huge amount of alimony to Derrick.

When Jackie first came to me, I ran her case through my system and I knew very early what her best- and worst-case scenarios were. I also considered what kind of timetable I should push: slow, medium, fast, ultra fast. Jackie was soon vesting in some big (though unknown to Derrick) stock options, so I wanted this case closed quickly. I convinced the court to schedule the settlement facilitation as soon as possible, which enlisted not a peep from my opposing counsel – a childhood friend of Derrick's who "specialized" in both criminal defense and divorce. Maybe this was going to be easier than I thought.

It was. As we proceeded to negotiate the settlement, I was almost disappointed by my opposing counsel's lack of preparation. He glossed over the stock options, which were buried in the massive document request he had sent to me (costing his client $300,000); he did not push the fact that his client probably had at least a $50,000 separate interest in the parties' joint IRA; and he did not require my client to secure her child support obligation (a potential $500,000 liability if Jackie died before the children reached age 18). It wasn't fair, but it wasn't my job to make this guy a better lawyer, nor could I ethically say anything about these shortcomings in the settlement.

It is true that the vast majority of divorce cases are ultimately resolved through settlement, by mutual agreement. But that does not mean that these settlements are anything close to fair. This particular case was so lopsided that Jackie feared we had taken advantage of Derrick, a decent guy just looking to move on with his life. "I worry about him sometimes," she said in our last conversation. And in that moment something within me began to shift. I was usually happy to bask in any victory – a win was a win, after all. But I knew what Jackie meant. The expression on her face was so downtrodden and disappointed that I couldn't even look at her.

Cases like this, with results so unnecessary if Derrick or his lawyer had just understood what to look for, would, in time, lead me to create a system for everyone to easily understand his or her rights, to organize and prepare their cases without having to rely blindly on their attorneys. But Divorce Declassified™, would be a long time coming; back then, I was only beginning to sense the creeping tendrils of disillusion. My win-at-all-costs method had given me all the trappings of success – money, clients lined up out the door, and a feeling of complete confidence. But there were times, ever so often, when I felt like a heartless machine, claiming expertise in perhaps the only area of the law where the heart truly matters– pumping with both tenderness and anger, and so often broken and battered by the time everything was over. Getting a divorce is just not a plug-in-the-numbers business. A realization was beginning to grow within me: my clients – and their exes – had needs and feelings that went beyond the bottom line, and far beyond what the current divorce system had to offer.

A Growing Unease

When I went to bed at night and closed my eyes, I started seeing the haunting glares of the ex husbands and wives from whom I'd won disproportionate alimony, custody and child support arrangements, houses, cars, and boats. Our culture holds that a lawyer with a conscience is a rare breed, more likely seen in storybooks – no one finds Atticus Finch in the phone book. But here I was, starting to wonder at the meaning of it all, though admittedly still married to my hard-hitting tactics.

It was during this period of unexpected doubt that my first multi-million dollar divorce signed on as a client. Maria and John had enjoyed a long and mostly happy marriage. Maria had raised their now-teenage kids while John built his multi-million dollar tech company headquartered in Santa Fe with assets spread across the country. But people change; John had a girlfriend; it was time to move on.

Before John had even retained his well-respected Santa Fe lawyer, I was out of the gate and halfway around the track. I hired the best business valuation expert in Albuquerque (if for no other reason than now opposing counsel couldn't), and filed an immediate motion for temporary division of income and debt, motion for immediate inventory of business assets, and asked to freeze at least one bank account that Maria worried John might liquidate. Then I dropped a request for discovery that would take them months to dig out from under, and filed a motion for a custody evaluation. The ball was rolling quickly and I enjoyed the rush of this massive pre-emptive attack.

I got a call from Maria on my cell phone early on a Sunday morning: John had been arrested for drunk driving. And not only that, his breathalyzer score was twice the legal limit.

"Perfect," I said. "This is perfect timing. I'll have an emergency motion for temporary sole custody on file by Monday morning."

There was silence on the line. Then: "David, listen to me. John is going through a rough time. His father has been sick and probably won't be around much longer. I think he's just completely stressed out."

"Well, you're going through a tough time too, Maria."

"Yes. We're all going through a tough time. This whole family's hurting."

Early Monday morning, Maria came into my office. We sat in my large conference room, and with the sun just coming up over the mountains she told me the whole story of their relationship. They had married young. John studied engineering at UNM while she got her degree in English. Her parents didn't like him at first. They lived in a little house south of Central and struggled together for years until the tech company finally hit it big. They had had a good life. She didn't regret a minute of it.

"So," she said. "I'm not really sure how to say this, but I don't want to do this like everyone else does. You're a smart lawyer, right? That's why I was referred to you, wasn't it?"

"I hope so."

"So, figure it out for me. We need to be divorced, that's true, but I can't have my whole family torn apart by this."

"Maria, listen, I'm your lawyer and it's my job to give you the *best* strategy to get you the *best* result possible." For a lawyer, this is the phrase that usually kills. It's our mantra, our Hippocratic Oath. But she wasn't listening.

"I know, and I appreciate that David. I know you would fight for me to the very end. But I need something else from you."

From downtown Albuquerque you can reach the foothills of the Sandia Mountains in fifteen minutes. Fifteen minutes later, if you hustle, you can be so removed from the world that the traffic looks like ants slowly marching. There's no sound from the city, and no other people around. Albuquerque is the largest, smallest city in the world.

That Monday afternoon, I roamed through the foothills and just let my mind wander. I tried to put myself in Maria's place, and for just a moment rejected everything that I had ever learned about the divorce and family law process.

At the end of the week, when she answered my call, John's lawyer was shocked that I wasn't filing an emergency motion. Instead, we spent a long time discussing to whom we could send our clients to work out their custody issues. With much trepidation on our parts, we decided we would send Maria and John to a child psychologist in Albuquerque, without the lawyers present, to see if they could reach an agreement on their own. The psychologist billed a fraction of our combined hourly attorney fees. I agreed to release our business valuation expert and hire a neutral evaluator, who would act as an expert to the court and report his findings to the judge. And then John's lawyer and I spent a long time creating a list of only the documents and information we really needed to properly represent our clients.

Now, it wasn't that this case was finally resolved with ponies and rainbows. There remained plenty of hurt feelings, crying, and arguing. We spent 12 straight hours in a mediation resolving all of the parties' issues, but by my estimation we had resolved this family's case in one-third the time and cost of a normal divorce case. The vast majority of their wealth had been preserved and both sides seemed happy with the outcome.

And, after everything was hashed out, instead of the usual post-settlement acrimonious parting, John gave Maria a hug and a quick kiss on the lips before they headed out of the conference room to begin their new lives. I stood amazed – instead of a scorched battlefield, this divorce ended with love and mutual respect. John and Maria had made each decision along the way *on their own*, with only the necessary input from their lawyers. It was so singular, so different in tone from my other cases – so much more humane – that the doubts and ideas that had been swirling within me for months finally came home to roost.

Starting to Find the Path

My quest for a better, less adversarial way to divorce began in earnest a year after John and Maria's case ended, when I headed to Dallas for a training workshop in collaborative divorce. At the time, this was a relatively new concept in my field. A Minnesota lawyer named Stuart Webb first coined the term in 1990. His aim was to create a way for couples to work out their separation outside the courtroom, thus reducing costs and acrimony. In his view, divorce was primarily a personal issue – one with certain legal ramifications, sure – but fundamentally about the intimate lives of two individuals.

In Dallas, I was introduced to a revolutionary way of handling divorce cases. At its most basic, if a couple chooses the path of collaborative divorce, they each hire a lawyer who has specialized training in this area. They effectively build their own team, a protected 'bubble' where everyone shares the goal of seeking a needs-based outcome. The couple is in control of the entire process – no courtrooms, no judges, no devolving a deeply-felt relationship into a pile of paper pushed back and forth by two lawyers. The method itself can be elaborate, but attorneys who specialize in collaborative divorce are invested in making it work. If negotiations break down along the way and the parties have to go to court – as, of course, they sometimes do – a whole new set of lawyers must be retained.

I was inspired! The divorce process for me had flipped – instead of a machine designed to get the biggest piece of the pie, it could now be a thing of real, human nuance. The adversarial model taught in law school was *not* the only way; there was a place at the table for cooperation, thoughtfulness, and mutual respect – all food for the heart. Collaborative divorce allows clients and their individual needs to drive the process, rather than leaving a faceless system at the wheel. With this new knowledge, the divorce process seemed limited only by the creativity of those involved.

I shone with the fire of the recently converted those first weeks back in the office after the conference. I would talk about the exciting possibilities of collaborative divorce with anyone who would listen. But my enthusiasm was a lonely island in the jaded sea of many of my colleagues. One afternoon in the courthouse, I was pleased to run into a friend and hero of mine. Jim was an old-school, hardcore divorce lawyer. Master of the nasty letter, a cool and thorough litigator – if you could hang with Jim you knew you were damn good. When he asked what I'd been up to recently, I mentioned I was getting trained in collaborative divorce, a field I thought had great potential for better serving our clients.

"I don't like it," Jim said without hesitation.

"What do you mean you don't like it? What's not to like?"

"It's just not what we do. We make our money going to court, filing motions, fighting. You take the fight out of it, what do they need us for?"

He was opposed to it on principle, which I found to be the attitude of many attorneys in town. A lawyer seeking a more peaceable path seemed an anathema, a slap in the face of pricey law degrees, long lists of credentials, and secret legal information closed to the general public. I got it. But I didn't care. As my experience with collaborative divorce grew, I began to see it as a first step into solving the awful grind of divorce. Often it was a great solution, and both parties walked away satisfied. But the fact remained: because collaboration required two lawyers trained in this arena, you are only as good as your opposing counsel. Lots of firms were beginning to offer collaborative divorce, but that didn't mean they excelled at it. If he or she had received shoddy training or weren't personally committed to the idea, the lawyer on the other side could derail the whole process.

After some years of offering collaborative divorce, this very real frustration led me to seek a purer method: single lawyer divorce mediation. This time I headed to Austin, Texas, to learn the ropes. Pure mediation was a revelation, a way of completely dodging the divorce process. Mediation offers several key advantages: first, it requires only you, your spouse, and your mediator – a neutral third party to help you resolve the issues in your case. This triumvirate means that the couple's needs – not the opinions or styles of their lawyers – are really at the forefront. Second, mediation strives for transparency between you and your spouse. There's no one else driving the process, so it's up to you to decide what is fair in your situation. Mediation is also a much less expensive solution as it avoids costly hearings, attorney fees, and unnecessary discovery. Finally, it is confidential. There is no public record of the parties' grievances.

For many couples, mediation can be a powerful tool for divorce. It is a way to circumvent the entire system. That said, for all its lofty principles of open communication and "working it out ourselves," mediation often has even the most hardened attorneys shaking in their shoes. Forget the discomfort of Negotiations class back in law school. A mediator finds himself smack in the middle of the heart-wrenching unraveling of two lives. There's no template, no spreadsheet here. You can't hide behind a pile of paperwork, a court's schedule, or a judge's ruling. A mediation demands handling *real* emotional fallout, having excellent listening skills, and knowing when to be a leader or take a backseat. It is skill-intensive and emotionally draining.

I hadn't been this uncomfortable since law school, and I loved it. There was real risk that my clients would never work it out, but there was also the ever-present possibility of achieving a certain frequency of communication rarely found in the normal process of divorce. The informal nature of mediation lets two people express themselves in a real, human way, allowing the heart to bleed if it must, cry if it must, and ideally set a course for a happier future.

Putting New Skills to Use

The word on the street: "What the hell happened to David Crum?" Some in my community wanted me to succeed; others hoped to watch me fail. So when a local attorney referred James and Cynthia to me, I wasn't sure of her motive – because this couple was an unholy mess: a successful tattoo artist and a real estate agent with a two-year-old daughter. Their problems ranged from money to sex to trust to where to live to how to raise their girl. This was the first time in my life that I sat in front of two people whose lives rested so completely in my hands. I knew then why so few lawyers did this type of work. It just felt *so* heavy.

In Austin, one of the instructors had advised, "No matter how brilliant you think you may be, sometimes you just need to get out of the way." So with James and Cynthia I got out of the way. I set the stage and outlined the consequences and then I let them talk. It is amazing sometimes what people can agree to when their lawyers take a back seat.

I would step in when things got too emotionally out of control, and I provided a clean map that could lead them to the resolution of their issues. We spent two half-days together hammering out things that would affect the rest of their lives. We built in some hard and fast rules, but we also built in flexibility. They both cried when they signed the final papers.

The Takeaway

I have now spent over two decades transforming not only myself but also the system that, in some ways, created me. In doing so, I've chosen to slough off many of the hardball tactics I learned in law school, refocusing my approach to emphasize what I feel is truly essential to the process of divorce: organization, emotional intelligence, and empathy. Having so tailored my approach, I've witnessed a shift in the overall tone of my clients' divorce proceedings. A combination of efficiency and humanity allows them the space to separate without destroying themselves, their financial health, or their families.

This is all well and good for my clients, but how does it apply to you? When the unfortunate circumstance of divorce crashes into your life, what exactly do you do? What steps do you need to take to lead you down the path of least destruction? Part II of this book will focus on a real-world approach for surviving your divorce. I will explore common missteps, provide surprising strategies for success, and offer organizational tools that can help you manage overwhelming feelings. These recommendations will build the foundation you need not only to survive your divorce, but also to embark on a new life.

Part II

Seeing
the
Light

Chapter 4

Avoiding Divorce Meltdowns – How to Practice Emotional and Wealth Protection

Divorce IS A declaration of independence with only two signers.

– *Gerald F. Lieberman*

In a moment a decision is made, a tipping point not unlike a plane leaving the ground or a wave breaking. This private moment when divorce becomes a viable option may be the culmination of months – or years – of unhappiness. It may be a sad, slow awakening or a dire reckoning. It may originate from you or your spouse. But this instant when divorce becomes more than an abstract concept is the beginning of a journey through rough waters. You are the captain – will you choose to steer with thoughtful intention or heedless passion?

The high emotional stakes of divorce deem this a question worth asking right at the outset. For even through the fog of rage, betrayal, sadness, and hurt, most of us can see the value in a divorce that doesn't swallow years and assets and your children's well being. So how do you accomplish this? By managing your divorce wisely right from the start. This is a feat with a high degree of difficulty because, even with the best of intentions, it is all too easy to tumble down the slippery slope towards divorce meltdown: decisions made out of anger or revenge, years spent in an out of courts, outrageous lawyer fees, kids traumatized. And you can be sure there is a system of cops and lawyers and courts that are more than happy to become intimately involved in your crisis. After all, divorce meltdowns pay their bills.

So what do you do? Let's begin with what *not* to do.

Only You Can Prevent Forest Fires

Here is an example of an all-too-common dialogue between a new client and myself:

Client: "David, I've been thinking through different scenarios. I've actually thought about this a lot. When you run through all the numbers, it's obvious that I should retain the business and we should share 50/50 custody. She can have the house. I want to be fair. What do you think I should pay in alimony?"

Me: "Ok, let's back up for just a minute. Have you told your spouse that you want a divorce?"

Client: "Well, not at this point. I wanted to see what my options are first. I'll get it all figured out and then I will tell her."

Divorces begun in secret can lead to disastrous results. It may seem obvious to share your desire for a divorce with your spouse *before* consulting an attorney, but for various reasons – fear, uncertainty, a desire to gain advantage – this often doesn't happen. One party begins to think seriously about divorce, jots down ideas and scenarios, and maybe talks to a friend who recommends a divorce lawyer. He then meets with this attorney on the sly and is instantly thrust onto a trajectory based entirely on that lawyer's attitude, practice philosophy, training, etc. I almost always suggest to my clients that they try to discuss the *fact* of the divorce before filing. While it is definitely not necessary to begin discussing the *terms* of the divorce, it is always best if there is as much transparency as possible around the process. This gives a couple many more options at the beginning of their case.

But what often happens is that the divorce is started by one person completely on that person's terms. Often they have already worked out some sort of resolution of the case in their head, and they have spent significant time working through the emotional issues surrounding their divorce. They can now see themselves single again and moving on with their lives. Of course, the other spouse feels totally blindsided, even if splitting up was something he or she, too, had considered. Not acknowledging this needed period of adjustment is one of the biggest problems I have encountered in the divorce process. The enlightened client knows he has to give the other party time to adjust, to get into an emotional space that allows him or her to start thinking about the possible terms of the divorce. The typical client simply doesn't understand why the whole thing can't be over tomorrow.

The worst example of this I ever saw in my practice was the case of Jerry and Kay. Jerry had come into my office after already filing his own divorce petition. Kay had been kept in the dark – not only about her inexorable divorce, but also about some nearly unbelievable facts about their relationship. At some point, Jerry had acquired a secret girlfriend. At some later point, Jerry had decided to have a doctor reverse his vasectomy and then promptly got his girlfriend pregnant. Yes, even I did a double take on this one.

When Kay finally learned the truth, she took the divorce meltdown to new heights. Of course she hired my arch nemesis Alicia Stone, who promptly began kicking Jerry's ass. I quickly forced the case into settlement facilitation, but Kay and Alicia would not budge from a very lopsided offer of settlement. Toward the end of our first long settlement conference that was clearly not going to settle, Jerry leaned over to me and said, "God, I just want this to be over with. Why the hell is she so pissed?"

A better choice than secrecy is to be up front about wanting a divorce, but this too is laden with emotional landmines. Whether one or both of you suspect divorce is a foregone conclusion, someone must first give it voice. In the moment of this, lashing out can seem like the only reasonable response to such a bold statement of rejection. And it's often the case that whomever is on the receiving end of the request for divorce will attempt to reclaim power with a threat: "Fine. But you can bet you'll never see the kids again." For a divorcing couple with children, threatening dire or unreasonable custody arrangements is a shot to the heart. But the fact is, these threats – whether they concern custody or unfair financial and living arrangements – are not based in reality and almost never come to fruition. They are simply a hurtful way of lashing out that sets the stage for an ugly ride. If it happens just let it happen ... then let it go without comment.

In my experience, a couple engaging in this first eggshell of a conversation should avoid discussing the terms of the divorce entirely. The reasons are twofold.

First, unless one of you is a divorce lawyer or judge, there is little real knowledge at play. You are talking about a vague situation about which neither of you is an expert. All over America, angry couples are arguing about settlement and custody resolutions in their bedrooms and kitchens – and none of it will *ever* happen. There's little to no knowledge about their legal rights, what good divorce or custody models look like, or what laws are state-specific for divorcing couples. It's a pointless exercise that can only lead to confusion and anger.

Second, this is a highly emotionally-charged moment. There are few people with the skill set to de-escalate their feelings in such emotionally difficult circumstances. Divorce is the last place people take the emotional high road. It's low, and the pain of it can feel like a siren call to work out your emotional issues. Whatever your pain is – whether it's from childhood or with your spouse or somewhere in between – now is not the time to let your wounded heart out of its cage.

Cops Make Terrible Referees

Words to remember: if you fight loud enough and long enough, someone will call the cops. And this is exactly what happened to a client of mine who was at the beginning stages of what developed into a horrific case of divorce meltdown. Jen and Chris were still living together, though both recognized their ten-year marriage was sputtering to a halt, when they had a heated argument in the kitchen one summer night. Who would move out? Who got the kids? Who kept the dog? Whose books were whose? It didn't take long for things to escalate, their angry voices carrying out the open windows. And then it happened: Jen picked up her phone to call a friend to see if she could stay over. Chris tried to grab it away ("No – please stay"), and in the ensuing tussle she lashed out, leaving a few small scratch marks on his neck. There was a knock at the door: "Open the door please. Albuquerque Police."

And here is where things commonly fall apart – when the cops show up, bad things always happen. If the cops are called, even if you just want them to be there as referees, more than likely someone will be charged with a crime, if not taken to jail. And then you're dealing with a criminal case where one spouse is a witness against the other and restraining orders are filed and all good will is lost. Even in the gentlest of domestic disturbances, the police may be forced to make an arrest. So when they showed up on this balmy night and asked a tearful Chris and Jen what was going on, of course they noticed the angry red welts on Chris' neck. And despite his protests that it was "no big deal, an accident," Jen was hauled off to jail for the night.

Jail is a menacing environment in which to reflect on how to handle your divorce. So it's no surprise that Jen panicked and asked me to file for a restraining order against Chris – a man who was actually a pretty good husband. She worried if she was viewed as the 'abuser' she would lose the kids, so filing for a restraining order was the only way to even the playing field. There were definitely some facts there that could allow me to argue for a restraining order. She had engaged the assassin, so what could I do?

At the hearing that ensued, there were mutual restraining orders issued against the parties. Then I really turned up the heat. Jen's family had tons of money to fuel the litigation and Chris essentially had nothing. So it wasn't difficult to starve him into a settlement that was beneficial to Jen.

Had the police not been involved at the outset of Chris and Jen's divorce, their journey would surely have been a happier one. Unless there is actual violence at play, calling the cops (or arguing so raucously that they are called for you) is never going to produce a good outcome. Certainly a restraining order can be necessary when there is real danger, but very often it is employed as a strategic play or revenge tactic. While restraining orders do provide protection, they also wreak havoc, including potential job loss and extreme antagonism at the beginning of a case. A smart lawyer can often create a softer solution, such as a civil no contact order in the divorce case, that creates the necessary space you desire while avoiding the nasty consequences of a full blown restraining order.

Doing It the Right Way

So what is the *right* way to handle your divorce from the outset? How can you avoid, at best, starting out on the wrong foot – and, at worst, ugly threats, visits from the cops, and general dysfunction? The two most important things to think about at the very beginning of the divorce process, at least from the emotional/relationship side of things, are: (1) an appreciation of the extreme emotional volatility that can sometimes rise up out of nowhere; and (2) a plan of how to de-escalate or remove yourself from the situation if a meltdown starts to happen. Almost inevitably when couples try to talk about a divorce, there are times when emotions get out of control. The whole point of the initial conversation is to set the tone for the divorce that is about to come, not to try to start working out the details of the divorce itself. There will be time for that later.

It's important, at the beginning, to communicate to your spouse that you would like the divorce to be amicable. You should tell him or her that although things are coming to an end you would like to preserve healthy relationships, keep your children healthy, and preserve your finances. Tell your spouse you want to be open and fair.

There will likely be nasty things said. One or both of the parties feel rejected and this is natural. If threats arise about custody, or alimony, or other things that will supposedly happen in the divorce, you will drive yourself crazy trying to argue about them. These things said out of hurt have no place in the real world of divorce law. I have lost count of the number of initial client meetings I have had in which I have to explain to the husband, that, no, the wife cannot keep the children from you. Or have had to explain to a wife that, no, the husband cannot refuse to pay child support. I spend half of the time dispelling the threats made from the other side. If a conversation devolves into this, or you feel emotions ramping up, you really should remove yourself from the situation. Always have a plan, a way to leave, a place to go when this happens.

One tool I have made available to people going into a divorce is something I call a "Divorce Truce." This is a document I drew up many years ago that sets out the proper course of conduct that everyone should follow while in the divorce process. I started out using it for clients who came to me for divorce mediation. I would have them each sign the document as a commitment to taking the high ground while we started to work through their issues. Later, I made it available to anyone who was going into the divorce process, whether they were my clients or not. The document is not legally binding, but it is a great way to turn your focus from the hurtful things in your relationship, to how you can get through this hurt in the most healthy way possible. *(You can download a copy with the link provided at the end of this chapter.)*

There are other, more ambiguous situations where a couple is uncertain if the finality of a divorce is what they desire. Given the right circumstances, there might be a chance for reconciliation. In this case, I often suggest that they work with a marriage counselor on something called a controlled separation. A controlled separation is an agreement you make with your spouse to separate for an agreed-upon period of time (usually not more than six months), and you agree to continue working on your relationship in counseling. Like a divorce truce, you also sign a document agreeing to standards of behavior, like not seeing other people, continuing to support the family financially, and co-operating with regard to ongoing custody of the children. If, after the six months, you have not made acceptable progress on your case, you have at least set the stage for a more congenial divorce.

Careful what you Say, Post and Write

Even under the best of circumstances, even for couples *committed* to handling their divorces sensibly, there can be bumps in the road. Often these bumps take the form of voicemails and social media. Keep in mind that all communications you have, both before and during your divorce proceedings, can come into evidence in your divorce case. This includes voicemails, texts, emails, Facebook posts, tweets, and blog posts. It should go without saying (but I'll go ahead and say it anyway) that threatening voicemail messages and emails, tasteless photos on Facebook, blog entries about your new boyfriend or girlfriend are all bad ideas. Recall Roger's less-than-friendly phone messages to his wife in Chapter 1. His rants probably felt satisfying in the moment, but were damaging and embarrassing when played in the courtroom. In this new world of constant connectivity, it can be easy to leave common sense behind – especially in a highly charged moment. But remember: everything you put out there can boomerang back at you and change the outcome of your divorce. Whatever you are saying and doing, imagine you are saying it or doing it in front of a judge, because that truly is the reality of it.

And this is a lesson that goes beyond rude voicemails. Any discussion of your divorce that you put in writing, no matter how seemingly innocuous, can often come back to haunt you. One client of mine sent an email saying he would "be OK with paying $2,000 per month in alimony." Innocent enough, right? But after negotiations fell apart and the case went to trial, opposing counsel raked this guy over the coals on cross-examination with this email. Every time my client said he couldn't afford the $2,000, opposing counsel would impeach him with the e-mail. Believe me, your lawyer would appreciate you putting nothing in writing about the terms of your case.

The Takeaway

There are myriad ways to hurtle down the path to a divorce meltdown – and very few strategies for avoiding it. But if you handle your divorce carefully and remain vigilant against the pitfalls we discussed in this chapter, you *can* get through this time with the least amount of damage possible. You *can* avoid the divorce meltdown. This is one of the most significant and fragile experiences of your life. Shouldn't it be approached with thoughtful intention?

****

Free Divorce Tool

Get Your Copy of My
Divorce "Truce" Document

If you would like a free copy of the Divorce Truce agreement that I encourage my clients and their spouse to use at the very beginning, please enter the following website address into the URL address line of your favorite Internet Browser:

www. 24HourDivorceLawyer.com/truce

This agreement will help you reduce the conflict and significant divorce expense created when spouses battle until the very end and everyone loses, except the attorneys. I really encourage you to use it.

Chapter 5

How a Referral and a Consultation Can Be Your Worst Enemies

EVERYONE IN TOWN knew John – the attorney with the solid gold resume and all the right things to say. You'd see him around town entertaining colleagues over linen tablecloths, a star on the local political scene, adored by the local news. He was a fixture, and if you asked around for a good divorce attorney, it was likely his name that came up. But here's the thing: John was a terrible divorce lawyer. He was great at networking, super at getting a seat at the table with the city's wheelers and dealers, but when it came to the down and dirty work of dismantling a marriage – he simply bombed.

John's ineptitude became especially apparent to me as his clients began to trickle into my office. Finding themselves six months, twelve months, and often much longer into their cases and stranded, these poor souls were coming to me to find a way out. Their retainers? Gone. Their phone calls? Rarely answered. So why hadn't they come to me in the first place? Why, in spite of his poor track record, was John still the go-to divorce lawyer everyone recommended? Simple. He had the awesome power of name recognition.

It's a strange and dangerous phenomenon I have observed over nearly twenty years of law practice. If you ask anyone for the name of a "good" lawyer he will do *anything* to give one. He will throw out the name of a lawyer he may have heard in passing, or seen on television. He may give you the name of the guy who represented his sister or brother or cousin or hairdresser, even when he knows nothing about how the attorney performed or what type of law the attorney practices. Why people seem to do this is unclear, but it appears that the ability to refer an attorney (and in fact most professionals) is something that is important to their own sense of worth. It makes them feel important. It makes them feel like they're helping. And as one last, painfully clear example of this, I once had a client who had expressed dissatisfaction with my own representation, and then referred THREE clients to me after his case was over.

Also remember that even when a qualified divorce lawyer has done a great job for a friend of yours, that case may have been completely different. Yours may require a completely different set of legal skills. While the referral may make the referring person feel great, relying solely on a lawyer referral can have disastrous results for your case.

Finding the ideal individual to help you navigate your divorce is a crucial initial step along what will be a challenging journey. It's not something to approach blithely, as this relationship will have a critical impact on you and your family going forward. Given this fact, shouldn't your search for the attorney who best suits your needs be approached with careful deliberation? Of course, but let's be realistic and talk about how this plays out in the real world. Someone who is in the emotionally fraught early stages of divorce is likely to feel overwhelmed at the thought of finding an attorney. It's hard to even know where to begin or what questions to ask. In the absence of a reassuring recommendation of a friend, many people are tempted to hire a lawyer through online directories or referral services. It is important to know that nearly all of these sources are simply paid placement advertisements. In other words, nearly all of these services are "recommending" attorneys because they have been paid to do so, regardless of that attorney's education, skill, or experience.

"Ahh...but," you say. "What about the State Bar? Surely my own State Bar will refer me to the right lawyer." Sadly you will need to re-think that assumption, as it is very likely that your State Bar also runs a paid referral service. If in doubt, simply ask them when you call for a referral. Often, some of the youngest and least skilled attorneys will register with the referral service through their state bars. I registered with the very same services when I went into private practice as a twenty-five-year-old, newly admitted attorney who knew virtually nothing about practicing law!

Online directories, and, in fact, most resources out there, both online and offline, that "help" you find an attorney are best used *after* you have become clear about the kind of lawyer you want, the type of personality, and the approach that would best fit your case. You can then peruse these listings with an educated eye rather than gamble your family's well-being on an internet search.

The importance of knowing what you want *before* talking to a potential divorce lawyer cannot be over-emphasized. Here's what normally happens at an initial consultation: you arrive at the lawyer's office and within an hour, in most cases, you have been indoctrinated into this lawyer's personality, opinions, and typical approach to divorce practice. It's not that clients are dumb or that lawyers are manipulative. For clients, the legal landscape is so foreign that most people do not understand the full range of their options, much less an appreciation of the power they can hold in their own cases. For lawyers, they simply gravitate to the approach that best fits either their financial model or the strongest of their legal skill sets. Clients can feel so vulnerable at this stage of divorce that anything may sound reasonable; they are just relieved to have someone on their side. So, if you find yourself in this first meeting with a bulldog litigator, a hardcore approach to your divorce begins to seem reasonable. Or if you happen to be meeting with a lawyer skilled in mediation – that approach will begin to feel right, too, even if it may be the very worst thing for your case.

As the saying goes: *If all you have is a hammer, everything looks like a nail.* Thus, litigators want to litigate, mediators want to mediate. Lawyers prefer to work within their wheelhouses and may resist, consciously or unconsciously, tailoring their approaches to your specific situation. This is not to demonize either of these styles, only to say that by going into a consultation blind, you risk agreeing to an approach that is not the best approach for your case, and ultimately losing control of your case entirely.

What a Great Attorney Looks Like

The fact is, like looking for a mate, there will be more attorneys who are wrong for you than right. There are now so many lawyers in every legal community that the possibility for a mismatch is high – higher still if you are uncertain of the type of service your situation demands. The reasons for this are myriad, but one complaint I often hear relates to lawyers who don't specialize in divorce at all. As crazy as it may sound, a lawyer does not have to even practice divorce and family law on a regular basis to handle your case. In fact, some lawyers who will offer to take your case handle only a few divorce cases per year as part of their overall practice. The problem with this is that law school does not prepare a lawyer to practice competently in this specific area, and it is only through training and experience that these cases can be handled properly. An attorney who invests all of his or her time handling family law cases is more likely to have the knowledge and experience needed to obtain your best possible resolution.

That said, even lawyers who handle a large number of divorce and family law cases may not have the skills necessary to provide representation as it relates to all of your divorce options. Today, family law has evolved to include a large number of specific sub specialties, like mediated and collaborative divorce cases. These types of cases require very specific training, commitment, and, honestly, a certain talent to handle them properly. If the attorney you are considering hiring does not have experience in these areas, you are greatly limiting your options.

What happens all too often is that people end up in the office of a lawyer who prides herself on aggressive litigation. But overly hard-hitting lawyers can sidetrack your case, set the wrong tone in negotiations, interfere with settlement, and drive up legal fees. More often than not, pit bull lawyers make the entire process uncomfortable for everyone involved and puts both lawyers and their clients on a defensive, confrontational track from the very start. Confidence, competence, and assertiveness are all valuable characteristics of a divorce lawyer, but you do not need a pit bull to handle your divorce. You *do* need someone who can say "no" when necessary in negotiating a good deal for you, not someone who bullies others.

A great attorney will be as aggressive as is necessary in the case. It is usually advantageous to start off the case in a civil fashion, offering a road map for a speedy resolution through settlement. A great attorney has experience in your jurisdiction (county), in your courthouse, and in front of your judge. Having that local experience ensures that your attorney knows the decision makers and how they make rulings on a daily basis. A great attorney will have a roadmap from the beginning that outlines possible settlement scenarios, clearly understanding how your assets and debts should be fairly divided.

These "great attorney" qualities should be a baseline, a place to start, as you tailor your search. Keep them in mind as you further refine what you require in a divorce attorney.

Matching the Right Attorney with the Right Process

Again, knowing at the outset what approach and skill set your divorce demands is crucial when hiring the right attorney for you. So how do you do this? How, in the mire of emotional turmoil, do you determine the best way to approach your divorce? Don't call a friend; resist going online. Instead, begin by taking a realistic assessment of your family's landscape. Are there serious custody issues? Complex financial disputes? Can you and your spouse still communicate in a reasonable way? Do you share some of the same goals for your divorce outcome (like preserving finances or successfully co-parenting your children)? Is domestic violence an issue in your relationship? The answer to these types of questions will have a major impact on the type of attorney and legal process that will best fit your case. And this will greatly narrow your choice of attorney.

To illustrate, below are three divorce scenarios that have vastly different lawyer requirements.

No Love Lost

It's hard to imagine this couple ever shared a life together – or even a sandwich. The husband wants out and he has a plan in place for both the money and the kids. This guy is the major bread winner in the family and is in total control. He's hired an attorney who specializes in 'men's rights,' a dubious distinction meant to attract a certain type of alpha idiot. The wife is slowly waking up after years of being under his thumb. When their son mentions dad's new girlfriend, all hope for a conciliatory split goes out the window.

In this type of scenario, a cooperative resolution is unlikely. This means, if you were the wife in this case, you shouldn't be looking for a lawyer who specializes in mediation or collaboration. It's not that you need a hard-nosed, super aggressive attorney, it's just that you need someone who is capable in court, understands what you need, can say "no" and can push back hard when necessary. It's important to understand that a lot of "threats" made by counsel and their clients are just a whole lot of posturing. The takeaway: in your search for legal counsel, look for someone you can imagine standing up for you in court and in a settlement conference. This should be someone who is smart and tough but is not willing to let the case get out of control.

The Financial Labyrinth

When a couple has a marriage that involves business ownership and/or the ownership of other complex assets, you need a lawyer who understands how to handle this unique class of divorce cases. Often, one of the spouses is in a position of control over both the finances and the information pertaining to the finances. It is critical, especially if you are the spouse who is not in control of the finances, to hire an attorney who can give you a clear picture of how to proceed with the case. This should include, among other things, a comprehensive plan to obtain complete information pertaining to the business and other assets, the possible retention or court appointment of a financial expert, and an ability to help you plot your financial future or put you in touch with someone who can help assist you in this area.

The takeaway: a lot of money is at stake here. Run away from any lawyer who cannot boil your case down into a few steps that will allow him or her to fully assess your case and can at least give you a basic understanding of how to envision your financial future.

We Still Care About Each Other But Have a Lot of Questions

I find this type of case both endearing and heartbreaking. This is the couple that realizes they cannot stay together but still care about each other. They have kids and some financial issues, and they are just not sure how to handle it all. This is the perfect case for divorce mediation with a lawyer who is not only qualified as a mediator, but who also understands the complexities of a custody case.

While I talk a lot in this book about taking back power in your divorce case, it is also important to understand that there are some issues that exist in your case that you may not realize are even issues (examples: Who claims the kids as a tax deduction? What happens if one parent wants to move out of state?). The right lawyer can help you curtail unnecessary and unanticipated pain through thoughtful mediation. The takeaway: if you are on decent terms and would like a healthy relationship after your divorce, hire a smart mediator who values your financial and emotional future, and who understands that the best interests of your children come first. In this way, you can untangle your lives out of court and with the least amount of long-term trauma for your family.

It does take work to find the right lawyer-client match, but it is well worth the effort. Of course, every divorcing couple is different and will have distinctive requirements. The key is to take a clear-eyed look at your situation before embarking on the search for your ideal divorce attorney.

All Attorneys Are Not Created Equal

Ok, let's assume you have taken a long hard look at your situation and have a good handle on the type of services and approach you require. There is now one last piece of the puzzle to consider. All attorneys who practice family law – whether they work alone or are part of a larger organization – function within the structures of their law firms. What most people do not understand is that the firm's philosophy, infrastructure, priorities, and overall vibe – will be critical to your case.

Fact #1: The number one complaint about lawyers, according to the American Bar Association, is that they fail to call clients back in a timely manner. Beyond this, in my own experience, I most often see lawyers fail to manage their cases properly. This is not about understanding the law or making legal arguments, it is the simple fact that divorce cases have a lot of information to manage: paystubs, custody schedules, home values, retirement accounts, health benefits, child support calculations, the list goes on and on and on.

Even smart lawyers can be terrible at case management. Lawyers do not study case management or law practice management in law school; they study theoretical law, so that's what they know when they graduate. Most do not know how to run a law practice. You need to be aware of this from the moment you call a lawyer's office to schedule your first appointment.

Notice how organized they are. Ask them how they handle calls and how many staff members they have. If you hire a lawyer who doesn't have a large enough staff, or doesn't have good case management procedures in place, it is unlikely that you will be happy with your representation.

Fact #2: Your lawyer's financial interest is most often in direct opposition to the speedy resolution of your case. This seems like a no brainer, but the more you fight and the longer it takes to resolve your case, the more money your attorney makes. Now, there is a fine line between being an advocate and someone who is just milking the client for fees. This is not to besmirch an entire industry, as there are plenty of excellent divorce attorneys who put their clients' needs first. But it's worth considering at the outset what is likely to happen if the best course of action for your case is *not* the best financial course of action for your attorney's practice. Is this a firm that encourages its staff to take a thoughtful, creative approach to each case? Or, is it more likely that time billed is the priority?

Pay attention to your instincts. It's a bad sign when a lawyer promises too much because the reality of any divorce proceeding is that there is a bit of give and take on both sides. An attorney who is not explaining to you what the other side is likely to argue, and is not outlining the possible downsides of your case, is doing you a great disservice. I'm reminded of a client who hired our firm after his wife, a high-powered CEO, packed up and moved to Aspen, Colorado, then filed a divorce proceeding in her new home state. It was clear that jurisdiction was inappropriate in Colorado, but the wife was clearly ready to fight and had hired a lawyer to try to scare our client into an unfair settlement with the threat of huge legal fees. And normally, this would be a strategy that might have worked, because jurisdictional issues at the beginning of divorce cases can eat up a huge amount of resources.

I assigned one of our top attorneys to the case, and she received the first lob across the net: a nasty letter from the wife's attorney. At this point our attorney had two options – the first and most obvious would be to respond in an equally aggressive tone, draft a motion to dismiss the case in Colorado, and get the court to decide jurisdiction, which we would have undoubtedly won after hefty legal fees. But our attorney, trained as a problem solver and focusing on the real needs of the client, did not go down that path and instead called the attorney simply to talk about the clients and their needs. She didn't even argue about jurisdiction. She simply asked if they could talk before things got out of hand. Opposing counsel was shocked. And I would imagine the opposing party was more than a bit irritated. Our attorney forced opposing counsel to talk about what her client wanted, insisting that they explore the practical outcomes of the case. The case was settled within 30 days with very favorable terms for our client.

This case was not a big payday for New Mexico Legal Group, even though it would have been for many other law firms. And I am sure that many law firms would take issue with how we handled it. The truth here is that there is a code of professional responsibility for lawyers that dictates that all lawyers zealously represent their clients. Some lawyers will use this as an excuse to run up legal fees in cases, claiming they are only protecting their clients. I read the rule to mean that I should zealously protect my clients in every way, including saving them money, time, and heartache, regardless of what that means to my fees. I suggest you find legal counsel who shares that same philosophy.

The Takeaway

Divorce is emotionally and financially challenging for all family members involved, even if both spouses cooperate fully throughout the divorce process. Finding a competent, compassionate, and ethical attorney who focuses his or her practice in family law and divorce and who will look out for your best interests is critical to resolving your divorce in the most positive manner possible. On the other hand, hiring an inexperienced or fee-driven lawyer who does not fully understand the divorce and family law process can result in a costly and prolonged conflict.

Your goal should be to go into the process with a full understanding of the legal and practical aspects of your case. The attorney you choose should be committed to developing the most positive outcome for you as possible—and as quickly as possible. The sooner your divorce is final, the sooner you can begin your new life.

Chapter 6

Navigating the Dangerous Roads of Your Divorce Options

YOU ARE RESPONSIBLE for your life. You can't keep blaming somebody else for your dysfunction. Life is really about moving on.

– Oprah Winfrey

Often, life's darker moments can boil you down to your essence; they hand you a mirror and say: "Here, this is who you are." Divorce is one of these moments. While it can be painful and traumatic, divorce can also be an opportunity to prove your mettle, to look into that mirror and like what you see. This is my challenge to you: reject the normal divorce disaster fueled by harsh emotions, petty desires, and blind trust in the "experts" – and instead simply take charge. It's time to break out of the typical divorce model, and it's up to you to do it. I know it's possible because I have seen many people do it. You can come out the other side of your divorce a better person and a better parent.

"But, David," you say. "I'm no authority here. I don't know the first thing about mediation, litigation, custody evaluations, or asset distribution. How can I be in charge?" The answer is that you can take control by educating yourself about all of your options, understanding which of them are going to be the best fit for your situation, and then – and only then – hiring a lawyer. While the typical attorney-client relationship has you flying at 30,000 feet in the air, white-knuckling the armrest back in coach, true transformation occurs when the relationship between yourself and your lawyer is redefined: you are now up front, the copilot on this journey. You know where the plane needs to go. Your lawyer simply flies it.

This outcome-based approach – where you have analyzed all your options and know the clearest path to achieving the result you desire – can be applied to scenarios as diverse as getting into college or buying a house. You can envision the endgame (dream school/ dream house) and know who to partner with (college counselor/realtor) and what you need to do to get there (good GPA/solid credit and down payment). In divorce, this same model applies. Just as you would study hard to get into the best school or save to buy an amazing house, your job as a client is to influence and work for the outcome *you want* rather than simply taking whatever comes your way.

That said, embarking on any unknown journey can be daunting. I was forever changed after ascending Mount Kilimanjaro in the summer of 2013. But in the months leading up to the climb, trepidation was all I felt, having never hiked beyond the Sandia Mountains of New Mexico. Completely out of my comfort zone, my only recourse was to learn everything I could about how to best experience the 19,341 foot climb. Along the way, I read testimonials by experts, guides, seasoned climbers, and novices like myself. I heard the horror stories: bone-numbing cold, devastating altitude sickness, and endless rain. I was inundated with information and realized that the climb itself was only one small part of this journey – the planning, training, traveling, and preparing was an enormous undertaking.

At the foot of Kilimanjaro, there were many different trails our group of twelve could have taken – some faster, some more costly, some more circuitous than others. For us, a positive experience meant achieving the summit without killing ourselves – literally and figuratively. So with the help of our vastly skilled guides, we chose a more moderately paced route. After the fifth day of hiking, awed by both the stunning views and grinding fatigue, the summit was in sight. And here we faced a decision: every website, every so-called "expert", advised waking up on summit day at 1AM in order to reach the peak at sunrise. This had been the plan all along, outlined in our itinerary, briefed to us by our lead guide, and this is what every other climbing team was doing on the mountain that summer. But we were tired. We had had a long day getting to basecamp, some of the climbers were struggling, and so the group called a meeting.

Without input from our lead guide, we discussed sleeping in a bit, but still leaving early enough to summit and get back to base-camp before sunset. Now, our guides were willing to do whatever we wanted. We could leave at one in the morning. We could leave later. We could decide not to leave at all, just give up and go down the mountain, but the guides didn't tell us this. Everyone always left base camp at 1AM so that was what we were going to do as well.

After our meeting, the group decided to reject what everyone else was doing and to leave base camp at 5AM. The result? Everyone was rested and strong on the trail. We watched the sun rise as we excitedly ascended; and all twelve of us made the summit feeling great, as we found ourselves at the top of the world's highest free standing mountain.

I mention this story to illustrate the following truth: in any challenging situation, be it climbing a mountain or surviving your divorce, you *must* maintain your power in the face of common experience and so-called experts. An outcome-based approach, tailored to the specifics of your circumstance, should be what is driving your case. Common sense and thoughtful preparation are more valuable than blind trust in any expert – including your attorney.

The Four Power Questions of Divorce

So here you stand at the foot of your own formidable "mountain." Like my experience at Kilimanjaro, there are several paths from which you may choose, divorce options that will provide distinct experiences and results. Below are the four questions you need to ask yourself while preparing for your divorce. Asking and answering them (in the following order) will help you determine which situation best applies to you and then set you on a course for resolution. Once you choose your path, with a bit of research, planning, and common sense, you can determine the process that will best suit your needs.

Question #1: Is my divorce uncontested?

Sometimes relationships simply don't work out despite our best intentions. If you and your spouse have agreed to disagree and move on with your lives, it could be that an uncontested divorce is a wise choice. An uncontested divorce can be done with or without an attorney. If you use an attorney, the attorney must technically represent one of the parties, but he or she is retained simply to draw up the agreement as directed by the parties, and to point out any possible legal problems with the settlement. So, if you decide your divorce is uncontested you then need to decide if you want to use a lawyer or handle your case *pro se* (meaning you represent yourself).

Of course, divorcing without the assistance of a lawyer saves legal fees. It can be as simple as going online or heading to your local courthouse and requesting an uncontested divorce packet. These documents are free and relatively self-explanatory. I will not tell you not to do this, because I have seen many couples do it effectively.

That being said, I have also witnessed many pro-se, uncontested divorce cases crash and burn. Why? Because this option only works well when there are limited assets, uncomplicated legal issues, and little to no custody conflict. If, on the other hand, you have tax issues, transfer of a home, questions about division of debt, or young children, what began as an easy option can result in many unforeseen future legal problems.

Ask yourself: Why do I think this is uncontested? What do we not agree about? Should we at least pay for a consultation with a lawyer to smooth out some of our questions or disagreements? It can be worth paying for a lawyer's advice if you run into snags – not for the purposes of litigation but simply to assist you in filing the papers correctly and lending authority to any outstanding issues you may have. (Note: some lawyers will be open to assisting with uncontested divorce, while others will not take such cases due to professional liability concerns.) If you can find a lawyer who will handle your uncontested divorce for a reasonable flat fee, I always think that's an option that should be seriously considered.

Uncontested divorce is popular because of its low cost, low conflict, and simplicity. If you have the luxury of pursuing this least complicated divorce option, it is definitely worth considering. And before you pay some online service for the forms you need, take a look at what your local courthouse has in terms of an uncontested divorce packet. Many of these online divorce services are simply using the same packet you can get from the courthouse at no cost, or very low cost, and then charging you a premium.

Question #2: If my divorce isn't uncontested, can it be mediated?

If you and your spouse have agreed to avoid a litigious divorce but serious disagreements remain, divorce mediation with a neutral third party may be the right path for you. In this scenario, a shared mediator supports and facilitates productive communication and a resolution of your legal issues. He or she provides suggested paths to resolution, encourages active problem solving, and has expertise regarding divorce in your state. Divorce mediation is confidential, less expensive than litigation (you are paying for one lawyer rather than two), and is especially valuable when there are children involved and lines of communication must remain open and amiable. The ideal result of mediated divorce is a mutually acceptable, tailored agreement that can then be presented to the court.

Mediation works best if you and your spouse have demonstrated a history of mutual respect and good communication skills. Ask yourself: can my spouse and I work together despite our very real differences? Can we both keep our eyes on our goals (financial well being, healthy kids, etc.) without becoming sidetracked by unproductive emotional struggles or painful memories? If so, proceed by seeking a mediator who has experience with family law – ideally, a divorce lawyer who practices mediation as well. In your search, look for lawyers or law firms that promote their mediation services as a main part of their practice. Mediation should not be a sideline, but rather another level of expertise the attorney you hire is actively promoting.

Warning: in many states, anyone can act as a mediator without any special qualification or licensing. Now, this is not to say that there are not some great mediators out there who are not lawyers, and it is very possible that a mediator who is not a lawyer can help you settle your case. Where I have seen problems is when even the best mediators, because of their lack of expertise in divorce law, write up agreements that have unforeseen and often disastrous consequences for clients in post divorce situations. Those issues almost always involve tax consequences, child support calculations, division of debt, transfer of real estate, and ongoing custody of children. If you decide mediation is right for you, do yourself a favor and hire a divorce lawyer who has expertise in mediation.

Question #3: If mediation isn't right for me, what about a collaborative divorce?

Some divorce cases have issues, both legal and emotional, that dictate each party should have his or her own legal counsel. These can include issues pertaining to alimony, highly contested custody issues, and other income/debt problems. In this scenario, collaborative divorce can be a smart path to resolution.

Attorneys trained in collaborative divorce have acquired a specific skill set that allows them to take your case outside of the normal divorce system. They will essentially build a container around the divorce process, which allows the parties to have ultimate control – as opposed to the whims of a typical divorce lawyer or the courts. Everything happens based upon the agreements of the parties, which includes everything from how and when information will be exchanged to how the parties negotiate custody and financial issues. Even with hot-button issues like complex financial situations, alimony, and custody disagreements, collaborative divorce tends to be more amicable, as there is a system in place for fair play and constructive communication. It can also be less expensive and time-consuming than litigation.

If this seems like the right choice for you, the first step is to seek a lawyer who is trained specifically in collaborative divorce. Because this is a relatively new area of the law, beware of lawyers who claim they can collaborate without really knowing what that means. Your town or city will likely have an organization of collaborative lawyers that can corroborate an attorney's qualifications and provide a list of those trained in this area. Collaborative lawyers will customarily want to work with other attorneys also trained in the same skill set. The organization or specific lawyer you approach should be able to recommend a number of people your spouse should consider.

A successful collaborative divorce will result in you and your spouse entering into a legally binding divorce settlement. You will likely never step foot in a courtroom. There is one caveat to using a collaborative divorce model in your case, however. If the case falls apart and you have to go to court, you will be required to find new legal counsel to represent you. This is one of the main tenets of collaborative divorce, which truly forces the parties and their lawyers to continue to work together. So if your case does fall apart in the collaborative process, you have lost the money you have already invested in the process and are essentially starting all over again.

Collaborative divorce works best when both parties have realistic expectations about the endgame; it's for people who believe divorce is not about getting everything they want or think they deserve. It's about preserving what is left of your family and finances and moving on with your life.

Question #4: If I cannot mediate or collaborate, how will I survive a litigated divorce?

Litigation starts when a divorce petition is filed and the parties have not agreed to a different course of action, like mediation or collaborative divorce. This is the least desirable type of divorce, but there is no need to panic. The vast majority of cases that begin in litigation will never go to trial, but will eventually end with a settlement agreement. It does mean, however, that the case will likely be much more contentious and expensive than other types of divorce proceedings. Also remember that there are many tools you can employ to help resolve your case even in the midst of litigation. You can ask that custody issues be mediated separately by using a psychologist or other custody expert who can meet with you and your spouse outside the presence of the attorneys. You can request an early settlement facilitation. You do not have to allow litigation to run wild in your case. You should also have a discussion with your attorney at the beginning of the case about how much the litigation may ultimately cost. Ask what steps you can take to control costs and legal fees.

Of course, finding the right lawyer for litigation will be key to a satisfactory outcome. What is the attitude that best fits your needs? If you have an aggressive spouse or opposing counsel, you will need to find someone who can stand up for you in and out of court. If your legal issues are complicated you will need a smart, organized attorney. Finding the right litigation attorney is so difficult because you won't really know if you've chosen well until you see your attorney perform in court. So ask yourself as you consult with various lawyers: *If I had to go to court and wasn't allowed to say a word, would I be comfortable with this person making my case before a judge?* If the answer is not one-hundred-percent yes, you need to keep looking.

The Takeaway

Once you've ruminated on these four questions, it should be fairly clear what option best fits your needs. If possible, talk to your spouse before taking any affirmative steps toward divorce. Envision a positive outcome for your case. Once you've got your map and your ideal pilot, you should be ready to fire up your engines.

Free Divorce Tool

I've created a **special 'Cheat Sheet'** for your use based on the '4 Power Questions' outlined in this chapter.

This resource is an easy to use, printable checklist showing each of the four major divorce types, including the advantages and disadvantages of choosing one over the other.

If you would like a copy for your personal use, please enter the following website address into the URL address line of your favorite Internet Browser:

www.24HourDivorceLawyer.com/cheatsheet

Chapter 7

The Blueprints For a Successful Divorce

WHETHER THE END of your marriage is a kind parting of ways, an acrimonious madhouse, or somewhere in between – it is bound to be emotional. But at the end of the day, divorce exists beyond matters of the heart: it is a legal process, one at which you can either fail or succeed. I've witnessed too many divorce meltdowns to let you head down the road to failure. And that is the purpose of this chapter: to give you a blueprint for everything that needs to happen for you to get through your divorce successfully and with the least amount of heartache and turmoil.

Think of it this way: divorce is both an ending and a beginning. As with all of life's transitions, there is a prescribed course of action that will achieve the best results. Like applying to college, changing jobs, purchasing a home, or any other major change you have experienced, there is, inevitably, a learning curve, deadlines, experts, people in positions of power ... and a lot of potential paperwork. Undaunted, you dive in because you know there's something you *want* on the other side of all of the work. In this case, it's the steady glow of moving on with your life, getting to the other side of your divorce.

You can do it. Let's get started!

#1. MONEY MATTERS

 ## The Least You Need to Know

Divorce begins with information gathering – what you have now and what you will need later. There are two key elements to keep in mind while compiling an overall view of your financial life: accuracy and timing. It is best to create a list identifying everything in your marital estate: all of your property (real estate, automobiles, collectibles), assets (retirement savings, investment accounts) and debts (loans, credit cards), along with their approximate values. It is best to have this in a modifiable worksheet that allows you to move the assets and debts into different columns. (**I have**

created a free asset and liability tool for you to use, listed at the end of this chapter.) If you don't have a value for, say, your house, discuss with your lawyer the best source for finding the value data. (Often there are less expensive resources such as market analysis rather than a formal appraisal.)

And everyone hates this word, but you do need, at least, a simple BUDGET for what your life will look like *after* your divorce. **(I have created a free budget for you to use, listed at the end of this chapter.)** While budgeting is rarely fun, this is the only way to determine what you will ultimately need from your divorce. What will your salary be? What will your expenses be? What debts will you carry? This doesn't need to be complicated, and obviously there are many unknowns, but creating an image of your post-divorce financial reality will go far in helping your lawyer create an effective strategy for your case.

I mention timing, because this is where I see so many divorces go off the rails. If you go into your first meeting with your lawyer with your financial information ready and organized, he or she will know exactly what to focus on, what records need to be found, what calls need to be made. If, on the other hand, time is wasted with partial information or lots of unanswered questions, you have already put your lawyer behind schedule for delivering a timely divorce. I am not exaggerating when I say you should begin compiling your financial information as soon as you know divorce might be a possibility – get copies of your crucial documents, tax returns, investment statements, bank statements. Having everything ready to go will save you both time and money.

 ## Making Your Wish List

With your list of assets and debts in hand, how do you think it should be fairly divided between you and your spouse? And what about other financial concerns such as alimony and child support? Ask yourself: if you could have your case settled today, what would you want? To keep the house? Or is having the cash from selling it more important to you? How much alimony will you reasonably need or be willing to provide?

Tell your lawyer early on what it is that you want and get her input. Most divorce cases are settled along an equal division of assets and debt. Of course, there are many permutations to an even split – she gets the house, he gets the portfolio/cars/whatever is of equal value. This is where your lawyer's negotiating skills and an early view of your goals will be crucial.

 ## Keeping Your Lawyer on Course

Remember: your lawyer may be the pilot, but you are the navigator, in charge of where this journey will take you. Lawyers are trained experts – and hopefully you hired a great one – but they are human, too, with other clients and pressures. It's up to you to make sure you're getting the services you are paying for.

With your worksheet as your primary tool, double-check that everything has been looked at and appropriately valued. Ask your attorney questions – "Do we have agreed-upon values for our vehicles?" "Do we have updated statements for his 401(k) account?" This is not to suggest that you badger your lawyer or inundate her with calls and emails. Just make sure that every major asset you own has been assigned a fair value. This is not the place for guesswork.

Warning! Warning!

Here's where things fall apart, and why I emphasize accurate and *early* information gathering. Too often, spouses will find themselves in a settlement conference ready to hash things out and move on with their lives. But there's a giant hurdle standing in their way: inaccurate values for items in their estate. Either the values vary widely (he says the condo is worth $500K; she claims it's only worth $300K) or one party has a value assigned to an item and the other does not. (In such a case, the settlement facilitator is likely to lean toward the value provided.)

Here's the rub: inaccurate or missing value data can lead to unequal settlements or unfair results at trial. Do the work early and you will reap the rewards.

#2. HOME IS WHERE THE HEART WAS

The Least You Need to Know

The question of who is going to keep the primary family home is almost always an important factor in a divorce negotiation. Besides being an emotional touchstone, the house you shared is frequently the most valuable asset in an estate. Whether one spouse plans on keeping the home, or you both agree to sell it, the first step is to settle on an approximate value of the property. Begin with a market analysis and see if you concur on the resulting figure. If you can't come to an agreement this way, look to a joint or court-appointed expert for an appraisal to determine a value. If selling the home is your plan, have an expectation of how long it will take to sell it and a reasonable prediction of a sales price. A reputable real estate agent familiar with your market can help you stay realistic.

Making Your Wish List

Who keeps the house, if anyone? You may want to remain in your home for any number of reasons: you have a great interest rate, there are young children who would feel uprooted by a move, or perhaps you have an emotional attachment to the property after years of good memories there. Keep in mind: if you do decide to fight to keep your home, be sure you can realistically afford it – covering the mortgage, property taxes, and maintenance on a single income is often a post-divorce shocker.

If, on the other hand, you have agreed to sell the house, who is going to live there while it's on the market? Who is responsible for getting the house market-ready? Will you split the profits 50/50? What if the house is underwater? Envision your best case scenario – and then tell your lawyer.

Keeping Your Lawyer on Course

Early on, your attorney should be able to get a sense from the opposing counsel if the issue of the family home will be problematic. Discuss your desires on this issue right from the start so he can create a winning strategy. Again, ask pertinent questions to make sure things are on track: "Do we have an agreement on the approximate value of the house?"

"Can we talk to opposing counsel to see how they would like to resolve any disagreement before we are in settlement or trial?"

Warning! Warning!

Here's what I've seen happen time and again: one party insists on receiving the home as part of the marital settlement agreement and gets it. She walks away from the settlement feeling victorious, but only for a brief moment. Because what her settlement requires is that she refinance the home to remove her spouse from the mortgage. This is something that is almost always required in a property settlement. To her surprise, after the divorce she discovers she doesn't qualify for a loan on her own so she has two unfortunate options: head back to court or lose the house.

Keeping the house as part of your divorce settlement and being unable to afford it, or not exploring the exact refinance requirements before you settle, can be financially devastating. In order to avoid this common landmine, do your homework early. If you want to keep the house, understand how much money you will need in order to afford it (this will likely directly affect the amount of alimony you ask for), and what you need to do to qualify for the new loan. Most banks will tell you exactly how much money you need to earn (alimony included) to refinance the home, and can also give you an estimate of your mortgage payment, including taxes and insurance.

#3. PUTTING YOUR CHILDREN FIRST

 ## The Least You Need to Know

The most important consideration here is what your child or children *really need*, and that comes down to understanding – and being honest about – what each parent can bring to the equation. If, for instance, the kids need a lot of help with schoolwork, or transportation to sports and other activities, a custody/visitation plan should be tailored to that. Key: the custody deal you seek should be informed by how your parental responsibilities were divided *before* the divorce.

Try to do everything in your power to keep a judge from deciding your family's custody arrangement. There are so many better options: using a child therapist to help keep the focus on the needs of the child, for example. Having a third party mediate this arrangement outside of courts and lawyers almost always results in a more positive outcome. That said, should your custody plan be determined in court, it is important to understand the standard the court will apply to making its decision. In my home state for example, the legal standard for custody is "best interests of the child," so all legal arguments are tailored around this standard. If you have children, one of the very first conversations you should have with your lawyer should involve a discussion of the legal standards that apply to custody cases in your state.

 ## Making Your Wish List

Throughout this book, I have advised having a clear vision of what you want in your divorce, but understand that when it comes to custody it simply cannot be about what *you* want. Custody must always be about what is best for your children. Now, that being said, there are certainly instances in which one parent is completely toxic to the children, and in that instance you will need to fight hard for primary custody of your children and to limit their contact with the other parent. However, I have found these cases to be rare, and in most instances the children are bonded with and want to spend time with both parents. You must think very carefully before ever attempting to limit your children's contact with your spouse. Remember that the law does not require someone to be a great parent, and that should never be the standard you apply in your case.

Your child is growing and changing each day. What will his needs be in three, five, or seven years? How can you anticipate the best way to provide for these ever-changing requirements? Do some research, talk to a child therapist. Enlisting an independent third party can change the entire tone of a case – from the push and pull of two parents who want to get the 'most' out of the custody arrangement to a refocus on the child receiving the 'best' custody plan.

 ## Keeping Your Lawyer on Course

At the outset, let your lawyer know that going to court will be the last resort in deciding your family's custody arrangement. (However, if you or the child are being abused, involving the court will almost always be required). Though passions run high when it comes to child custody, it's up to you to set the tone, not your lawyer. Encourage her to begin custody negotiations in an even-keeled manner.

From the beginning, ask your attorney to ascertain exactly what the differences are in the custody positions of the parties. Is there an issue over the child's primary residence? How will visitation be scheduled? Can the child be left with a new girl-friend/boyfriend? With this information in hand, you can begin to formulate a strategy to deal with these issues effectively. If you are close you may be able to negotiate a deal through your lawyers. If you are not so close you might consider using a third party mediator to help. If you are terribly far apart and your spouse is clearly not interested in a child-based resolution, you may need to let your assassin loose.

Warning! Warning!

People in the thick of custody negotiations have a tendency to rewrite history. For instance, the primary breadwinner, mother or father, working 80 hours a week, now decides he or she is going to fight for a 50/50 custody arrangement. This person has never in this kid's life been the main parent, but now is going to pull out all the stops for equal time. I cannot tell you how many times I have been on the other side of this case. The result? We fight it out until the end and the court awards the exact custody I offered at the beginning of the case, something in the best interest of the child that makes sense considering the lives and responsibilities of the parents.

Be realistic about how much time you will be able to spend with your child once the divorce dust settles. If you have a demanding career, it may be best for the child to enjoy quality weekend visits with you rather than 50/50 shared custody. It's ok. You do not have to have 50/50 custody to be a great parent.

#4. LOVE YOUR CHILD, SUPPORT YOUR CHILD

 The Least You Need to Know

Child support payments are monies that go directly toward paying for the needs of your children – clothes, food, shelter, education, etc. Payments are made, in most cases, until the child reaches his or her 18th birthday or graduates from high school. Every state has its own formula for calculating child support, based on the number of children, both parents' gross incomes, and primary, joint, or shared custody arrangements, among other considerations. Find your state's child support calculator online and learn what expenses can and cannot be included.

The information needed to calculate child support is fairly straightforward. If you are the custodial parent, the parent receiving child support, be sure, however, that you have an accurate understanding of your spouse's income. Are there other earnings in addition to his or her primary employment? Dividends? Rental properties? Overtime? A second job? An accurate accounting will ensure a fair child support payment.

Making Your Wish List

Child support is normally straightforward and relatively non-negotiable. The custody arrangement you are seeking will determine how your family's resources are split to provide for your children. As always, it is wise to do everything in your power to come to an agreement outside of court. There are certainly times when child support amounts are open to interpretation, but you should be very careful in this regard. Often, the amount of child support you might save through litigation will be grossly overshadowed by the amount of legal fees you will spend to achieve this small "victory." When it comes to child support, always stay focused on the bottom line.

Keep in mind that child support payment orders are almost never final orders and that they can always be reviewed by the court in the appropriate circumstances. This is especially true in situations where one of the party's income changes significantly.

 ## Keeping Your Lawyer on Course

Help your lawyer help you by providing her with the information necessary to establish your income accurately. Pay stubs, tax documents, and any other proof of income will be helpful to your attorney in negotiating the appropriate amount of child support.

 ## Warning! Warning!

There are several possible pitfalls when it comes to child support. As touched upon above, inaccurate income information (especially for people who own businesses) can prevent your children from receiving the appropriate amount of financial care. Another common mistake is failing to secure child support with a life insurance policy. If your children happen to be very young at the time of your divorce, there is a greater chance that the paying parent may pass away over the next five, ten, or fifteen years. If your state allows it, you should try to ensure that payments continue even in the event of death by securing a life insurance policy to support these obligations.

Finally, depending on your state and your particular circumstances, you may want to obtain a wage withholding order (known in some states as a wage garnishment). This requires the non-custodial parent's employer to automatically withhold a set amount in child support for each pay period, a system that goes a long way toward insuring these monies actually get paid.

#5. SPOUSAL SUPPORT

 ## The Least You Need to Know

Alimony payments are monthly disbursements one party pays to the other after a divorce, most often when one spouse earns a significantly higher salary than the other. Again, accurate income amounts will be key to reaching a spousal support agreement. Check to see if your state has an alimony calculator – these can provide a good place to start your negotiation, but many states do not have rules that set exact amounts for alimony.

Both sides must reach an understanding of the needs of the spouse who will be awarded alimony and the ability of the other side to pay such alimony. For this reason, creating accurate post-divorce budgets for both parties is crucial toward achieving a mutually agreed-upon amount.

 ## Making Your Wish List

As a divorce lawyer, my number one focus in alimony cases is always on the parties' budgets. For me there were only two issues: (1) what is the need of the person receiving alimony, and (2) what is the ability of the person who is paying to actually pay? I suggest that you make these two questions central to your own approach, but always in the context of your own state's laws concerning alimony.

From the perspective of the person paying alimony, it is important to understand that alimony is taxable income for the recipient and tax deductible for the person paying. This fiscal reality should be taken into consideration when deciding how much support you request/offer to pay. This means that alimony payments are never a dollar for dollar transaction. If you are in the 25% tax bracket for example, every dollar you are paying to your spouse in alimony is really costing you seventy five cents. I always remind the person asked to pay alimony, whether my client or not, that their spouse was once a person they cared about very much. They cared enough about the person to marry them, and often to have children with them. Despite the bad feelings that are now present, I ask people to remember these facts when they think about their spouses going off into the world on their own.

 ## Keeping Your Lawyer on Course

Have an early discussion with your lawyer about your expectations, based not on emotion, but rather on expected property division and incomes. Prepare your budget and ask him to request a budget from the other side. Your goal of how much to pay or receive – and for how long – should be reasonable to yourself and in the eyes of your attorney, who should be experienced enough to tell you if your alimony hopes are realistic. Inquire: is it worth asking for a certain amount and risking going to court, or is it wiser to try for a middle ground or settle for what is offered? A smart attorney will understand your BATNA (best alternative to a negotiated resolution) and apply this to your strategy. Simply put, your lawyer should be able to tell you your worst and best case scenarios, and that should be instrumental in how you deal with your alimony issue.

 Warning! Warning!

There are three common mistakes clients make in alimony cases: (1) They try to take their spouses for the very highest alimony amount possible. I have often seen this end in court with high legal fees and the court very often awarding less alimony than what was requested. (2) They try to pay far less than what is reasonable. Again, with these lowball tactics, I have most often seen the court award higher amounts of alimony, but only after the parties have spent large amounts in attorney's fees. The money spent by both sides in these cases, by the way, could have been used to reach a more reasonable settlement. (3) One of the parties overpays (because of guilty feelings) or requests far less than what is appropriate (again because of guilty feelings or even more often because they do not realize how much money they will need after the divorce is over). There is a sweet spot that reflects a real need on the part of the person receiving and the ability of the other party to pay. A fair-minded negotiation with reasonable expectations, guided by your attorney, is unquestionably the approach you should be taking in your alimony case.

Also, similar to the child support issue, if you are the alimony recipient, be sure to explore securing your alimony with your ex's life insurance policy or some other asset if that is allowed under the laws of your state.

And finally, know that legal fees spent in obtaining taxable alimony are tax deductible for the recipient. This means at the end of your case your lawyer should provide you with an itemized list of time spent on your case to obtain alimony. Depending on your situation, you may be able to claim that amount as a tax deduction.

#6. RETIREMENT: THE FUTURE IS NOW

 ## The Least You Need to Know

If you and/or your spouse contributed to retirement accounts during your marriage, such as 401Ks or IRAs, this is yet another piece of your marital estate that needs to be divided. Also, a pension earned by either party during the marriage is considered a joint asset in community property states, and is likely subject to division in other states as well. 401Ks and IRAs are relatively easy to divide or bargain with, as they have a specific value. A pension, however, can be trickier. There are complicated rules about how these assets can be divided and when the interest should be paid to the other spouse. Often an expert may be needed to calculate the present value of the pension if the parties are seeking to equalize the value at the time of divorce.

The most important point here is to do your homework early and make sure your attorney understands the issues pertaining to the division of this asset. I cannot stress this enough, often a pension is by far the most valuable asset a couple owns. If you have any doubt about your lawyer's ability to deal with this asset you should seek a second opinion immediately.

 ## Making Your Wish List

It may be tempting to procrastinate dealing with this issue. After all, it can seem so far removed compared to more pressing concerns such as child custody. But you should not, under any circumstances, settle your divorce case without specific agreements as to your retirement accounts and pensions.

Keeping Your Lawyer on Course

Identifying the retirement accounts/pensions in your marital estate is part of the standard discovery request that your lawyer will send to the opposing counsel. Double check with her that this request was made and, once both sides have the accurate values in hand, discuss with her what you want so she can begin the negotiation.

 ## Warning! Warning!

Dividing up pensions can often be problematic, especially if you have retained a lawyer who is not experienced in this area. At the very least, you should know the answer to the following questions: (1) What is the law in your jurisdiction regarding payouts of pensions? (2) Specifically, do payments begin at the earliest retirement date or upon actual retirement, and is this negotiable? (3) How will the survivor benefit be handled? In other words, what will happen if the spouse with the pension dies? Will payments continue, and if so, who is responsible for bearing the cost of the survivor benefit premium while the pensioner is still alive?

Often, the lawyers are required to submit orders to the organization in charge of the pension to ensure that benefits are paid according to the divorce decree.

These orders are commonly called QDROs (Qualified Domestic Relations Orders). It is not uncommon, however, that the QDRO will be rejected for various technical reasons and will need to be re-submitted by the lawyers for approval. You *must* stay on top of your lawyer until this is completely finished.

#7 TAXES: AS IF DIVORCE WEREN'T HARD ENOUGH

 ## The Least You Need to Know

How your divorce will affect your taxation can be divided into two categories: before your divorce and after. **Before**: Are there any outstanding taxes due? How will this debt be divided among you and your spouse? How will you handle your taxes for the year in which you are getting a divorce? **After**: Who will claim deductions for the children? Are you reporting any alimony received as taxable income? (This rule does not apply to child support received.) Does it bump you up to a higher tax bracket? If you own a business together, who will be liable for any tax issues that may surface after the divorce?

Making Your Wish List

Many tax issues come down to who will claim certain deductions, primarily for the children. Federal law provides that the custodial parent claims the deduction, but some states allow it to be awarded to the other party or split by the parties. If you are the custodial parent, you may not want to even address this issue with the opposing party, as the child tax deduction will automatically default to you under federal law.

If you elect to change your name, be sure to request a new social security card as soon as possible. The Social Security office and IRS must have a matching name in order to process your tax form. You should also ask your lawyer if your name can be changed as part of your final divorce decree. This is often a much easier and quicker way to restore your maiden name than the usual name change process.

 Keeping Your Lawyer on Course

Make sure your lawyer is aware early of your wishes and assumptions concerning child deductions. Any other taxation sticking point that you suspect may muddy the waters – back taxes owed by you, your spouse, your business, for example – should be put on the table as soon as possible so that your attorney has a clear picture of what she's fighting for.

 Warning! Warning!

Dealing with tax issues can be a headache – one most of us would like to avoid. The primary pitfall here is that people tend to be vague about what deductions they will claim due to a lack of understanding or simply not wanting to deal with the issue. There may also be past tax liabilities that are tempting to sweep under the rug during this already stressful time. Don't give in to that temptation – bringing all of this to your lawyer's attention can curtail future, bigger headaches.

#8 THE BIG PICTURE

 The Least You Need to Know

Throughout your divorce, you should maintain an aerial view of your overall strategy and timeline. These things will shift and change, but if you take time to keep your head above the minutiae, you can keep overwhelming feelings at bay.

As the co-pilot on this journey, it's your responsibility to know what you want and how to get there – and who can help. Your lawyer is your partner, but there may be others who will be crucial to achieving your best outcomes – financial experts, mediators and therapists. Look to your community and take advantage of the many resources available.

 ## Making Your Wish List

A great tool to keep you on track is understanding your BATNA (best alternative to a negotiated resolution) for *everything* – from child custody to who gets the record collection. Refer to the seven points above and create a document listing the *best* outcomes (according to your lawyer) that you could receive if your case proceeds to trial. Then make a list of the outcomes that may not be exactly what you want but that you could live with. This will go a long way in helping you determine a fair settlement of your case.

 ## Keeping Your Lawyer on Course

You and your lawyer should create a comprehensive checklist of everything on your divorce table. Ask him: What is the best strategy for achieving each of these desired outcomes? What is the specific timeline for scheduling a settlement?

Warning! Warning!

Congratulations! The day of your settlement conference has at long last arrived. You and your lawyer head into battle...and everything falls apart. Going into settlement without a clear understanding of where your case should settle is a big mistake and can lead to an expensive trial. You and your lawyer should know *before* going to settlement the various permutations of the negotiation and be prepared to deal with them. Don't panic when you hear the other side's initial offer. Very often, cases settle a long way away from the initial offers of each side. But it does take patience and the ability to stay calm.

It can certainly feel great to walk away from settlement negotiations without a deal and yell, "I'll see you in court!" but that may be the most expensive phrase you ever utter. Not understanding the financial consequences of going to trial is perhaps the most ruinous divorce pitfall of all.

The Takeaway

The above eight issues are a rough blueprint of what you should be thinking about as you head into your divorce. Some may apply to your specific case, while others may not – and all can be delved into more deeply. But now you have an idea of the road ahead and can conceive a winning strategy with the help of your lawyer and the tools found at:

www.24HourDivorceLawyer.com

With light now shed on these crucial elements of divorce, I hope you feel empowered on your journey toward life on the other side.

Your Free Divorce Tools

I realize some of this can be overwhelming, so I've created some free tools to make your life and your divorce easier.

If you would like a copy for your personal use, please enter the following website address into the URL address line of your favorite Internet Browser (use lowercase only):

Modifiable Budget Worksheet
www.24HourDivorceLawyer.com/budget

Modifiable Asset and Liability Worksheet
www.24HourDivorceLawyer.com/worksheet

Chapter 8

Throwing Your Kids Under the Bus (The Myth of the "Custody Battle")

FINN'S PARENTS HAD spent the better part of the year locked in a heated custody dispute over their ten-year-old son. Now, just before the holiday season, a court-appointed child psychologist had completed her work. A conference was set to go over the results with Josh and Kay and their respective lawyers. Josh came from work, looking authoritative in his lab coat;

Kay wore an arsenal of tasteful separates, nothing too sexy but not frumpy either. They sat at the long table, sipping water for something to do as the psychologist pulled out her notes. The psychologist began, taking time to look each parent in the eyes. "Kay. Josh. I've spent the past few months learning about your family and thinking about how best to recommend moving forward. But before I get into that, I have to say something to you both." There was silence in the room.

"My God, what is it? Kay said. Why do you look so serious?"

The psychologist paused for a moment, looked down, then looked straight at both parents. "Your son, Finn, is in a hell of a lot of pain." I literally did a double-take when I heard this, snapped my head back to look at the psychologist again, then turned my attention to the parties. Kay looked like she'd been punched in the face. Josh just sat there blinking. And within minutes both parents were literally sobbing, or at least doing their own version of sobbing. I handed Kay a tissue. Josh excused himself from the room. Josh's lawyer gave me the classic shoulder shrug.

Now, I will be the first to admit that my client had been just as unreasonable as Josh over the whole course of the case. Both of them had insisted on dredging up every little infraction, every small hurt, every mistake that the other had ever made during the marriage. While I tried to dissuade her, Kay wanted a war, and sometimes, as a lawyer, you've got to have your client's back even when you don't necessarily think she's taking the right course. So we went to war.

We dragged Josh's DWI conviction into the light, and opposing counsel dug up records on Kay's treatment for depression. Kay accused Josh of infidelity (which was actually true). Josh claimed Kay was reckless with their finances (which was also true). Kay claimed Josh had an anger management problem. Josh claimed Kay was psychotic. Each maintained the other was an unfit parent.

I felt the case was getting completely out of control so I called opposing counsel and asked if we could agree to stop sending letters and filing motions and send the parties and their son to a formal custody evaluation. "I thought you'd never ask," he said.

The custody evaluation put everyone on their best behavior for a while. This is a process that happens in a lot of states. A child psychologist is appointed by the Court to evaluate and recommend the best custody arrangement for the child. This can be a long and expensive process, and typically involves psychological testing, parent-child observations, and interviews with other people who are involved with the child, like teachers, family friends, and therapists.

As the months passed, Finn was unwittingly treated, by both of his parents, as a prize to be won – which, in fact, he was. Kay would tell me time and time again that when she questioned Finn, he insisted that he wanted to live with her, and that, really, he didn't want to see his father at all. I told her to stop questioning Finn.

Simultaneously, opposing counsel wrote me letters indicating that Finn had told his father he wanted to be with *him* full time. Opposing counsel even filed a motion for an *in camera* interview with the judge, which meant he wanted the child to express his wishes to the judge in the judge's chambers. I opposed the motion and the motion was denied.

Now, nearly a year later, the one person who truly understood this case was bringing her considerable intellect to bear on both parents. In the fading light of the conference room, she continued: "Finn understands that you both want full custody of him, and has come to the conclusion – despite my advice to the contrary – that eventually he will be forced to choose between you. His dread of making such a decision has directly resulted in his poor performance in school. He's depressed. He feels disconnected. He's afraid and he feels incredibly unsure about his future. Are you not seeing this? Do you not see that every one of your child's problems is stemming from this fight over custody? I know that you don't want to hear this, but he loves you both. He wants to spend time with *both* of you."

Never in my entire legal career had I experienced such an immediate change in the posture of a case. It was Josh who spoke first. It was something like, "What can we do to help him?" And then everything changed.

Suddenly we were able to start talking about joint custody, about what kind of timesharing would work for *Finn,* about how they could work together to help their son succeed. And I swear to God, we walked out of that psychologist's office with a complete parenting plan and custody agreement. We did in two hours what we had been unable to do for nearly twelve months.

Why Wait to Start Focusing on the Kids?

This is what I have never been able to understand in custody cases. Some clients insist on fighting over custody when a fight is not really warranted. And I'm talking about *mean* fighting, the kind of fighting that would make most parents cringe. The parties go down this road until they are completely exhausted and beaten up, and then, and *only* then, do they realize what they are doing to themselves and to their children.

For Kay and Josh it took a neutral third party to wake them up to the fact that they were hurting their own son with no justification. So I always ask, why do people have to suffer first, only to realize later (sometimes too late) that there is a better way? This is one of the major reasons I have written this book.

In my practice and around the country, I hear people constantly using the term "custody battle." While it may now be part of the divorce parlance, this so called "custody battle" is a myth, and the idea that this is somehow a noble cause is a complete disservice to families all across the United States. I will say it again, there are only *rare* cases that justify all-out litigation over the issue of custody. Most cases are, in actuality, all about parents who cannot reconcile their own feelings about their divorce, and cannot put the interests of their children ahead of their own emotional issues.

Let's look at the story of Kay and Josh to illustrate some common child custody blunders. First, both parents involved the child in their divorce. The truth is, children will commonly tell both parents that they want them to be their primary parent. Even so, I have too often heard both parents say this in a custody case to justify their claim for primary custody. It is both sad and disturbing. The child struggles hard to please both parents, whom he loves and still wants to be part of his life. Then the parents use this as ammunition in court. Kay and Josh did not conceal or even mute their mutual derision in Finn's presence, and even directly complained about one another to the 10-year-old. This puts the child on high alert, worrying that one or the other parent might be stripped from his life. If you think that your children do not pick up on both your direct and indirect communications about your spouse you are sorely mistaken.

Shielding your child as much as possible from negative feelings and the details of the custody negotiations is both kind and wise. One recent study shows that 25 percent of adults whose parents divorced when they were children have significant social or psychological issues, compared with 10 percent of those who did not experience a divorce. While this figure may be disheartening, all is not lost: the study also notes that children fare better down the road if their exposure to parental conflict during a divorce is limited[2].

The other major problem was that Kay allowed her anger at Josh's affair to immediately set the tone for the proceedings. This is a perfect example of the type of legal dilemma that can be driven by a client. Kay had proof that Josh had been seeing someone while they were separated. In New Mexico, that's not really a big deal, at least in terms of the divorce. We are a "no fault" divorce state and courts do not seem to care about these things at all in the legal context of divorce. Kate also knew that Josh had sometimes left Finn with Josh's girlfriend when he had to work late. Again, not a huge deal. *But,* in doing some investigation of Josh's girlfriend I had found out that she had been recently convicted of drug possession ... marijuana under one ounce.

Now, was the girlfriend's misdemeanor drug conviction a cause for concern? Sure. But it was

---

[2] Arkowitz, Hal and Scott O. Lilienfeld. "Is Divorce Bad for Children?" Scientific American, 2/14/13.

something that needed to be handled in the proper context. As far as we could see, the girlfriend had a good education and good job. Finn seemed to like her. To me, the drug thing was something that needed to be addressed, but as a normal part of the custody case. It did not need to lead to World War III.

On the other hand, could my client make a legal argument that Josh was placing Finn in a potentially harmful situation? Sure. Could she legitimately file a motion for temporary sole custody? Well this was certainly an issue that could be legitimately argued to the court. And Kay insisted that that was what she wanted to do.

So we filed the divorce petition making allegations that Josh was not currently a parent fit for custody, and we filed a motion for temporary sole custody of Finn. In the end, the allegations did far more harm than good for the case.

The takeaways here: do not talk negatively about your spouse in your child's presence. Save heated discussions for a private meeting or phone call (or better yet, don't have them at all); and don't "talk" to your ex through your child ("Tell your dad to send some clean clothes the next time he drops you off." "Let your mom know I would appreciate it if she's on time for our next exchange.") Simply let your child know that both of you are working hard to figure it out and that he is very much loved. If you feel it would be helpful for your child to talk to someone, enlist a reputable therapist, not a judge. Never put your child in a situation where he or she is asked (or even feels like he or she is being asked) to choose between the parents. That situation (real or imagined) is toxic to the child.

In the end you may ask, how *do* we decide what kind of custody arrangement is appropriate? Most lawyers will say something like, "It really should be decided on a case-by-case basis," or "Every case is different." While true, let me share a few things I have seen in my nearly two decades of handling custody cases. The first is that most children need and want a primary place to live. While it is certainly possible for divorced parents to share 50/50 custody of their children, in the vast majority of cases, I have not seen this work. This is a situation that becomes very hectic and stressful for the child, and I have heard many children describe this arrangement as "living out of a suitcase," or being on "permanent vacation."

Please remember that you do not have to have your child half of the time or a majority of the time to be a great parent, or to have a positive impact on your child's life. It's all about the *quality* of the time you spend with your child. It's about being present, listening, supporting, and advising to the best of your ability.

With that in mind, it is an absolute must to be completely honest about how your life, personal and professional, fits into the lives of your children. When the dust of the divorce settles, how will you be there to support your child? Are you the person to help with homework or is that not your strong suit? Do you have time to take your child to sports practices and games? Will you be there when the child has to come home sick from school? Are you the parent who can take your child school shopping, make sure she gets to school on time, is picked up on time, and has everything else she needs to thrive? The most contentious custody cases I have seen usually have one thing in common: one or both of the parents have a completely unrealistic idea about how they will fit into the life of their child. Much time and many resources are then spent until the parent, or parents, are forced to face that fact.

Also remember that custody determinations are rarely final orders of the court. Children grow quickly and their needs are ever-changing, and as these things change so do the mechanics of parenting plans and custody schedules, whether this is done formally or informally. There's no need to fight to the death for an arrangement that will likely be changed many times over the course of your child's life.

Thinking Outside of the Custody Box

As you know by now, the tendency of most lawyers in custody cases is to argue full-out on behalf of their clients. That, in and of itself, isn't a bad thing. It's what your lawyer is trained to do and what you are paying for, after all. But custody cases are the exact type of situation in which the very training your lawyer has received can derail your case. Let me give you an example.

A common complaint in custody cases is that one of the spouses drinks too much. This may be true or untrue. Now, based on his or her training, the lawyer on the other side of this allegation will look for external evidence, some neutral proof of this fact, to evaluate whether it is important or not. The lawyer will look for things like DWI or other criminal convictions related to alcohol, employment problems concerning alcohol, prior treatment, or any client admissions. The lawyer will also be interested in any witnesses who might testify about this issue. And guess what? In the majority of the cases, only the husband and wife really know the truth.

When I worked from assassin mode, I would take a look at these allegations and assess whether there was something out there that could hurt the client. The client, by the way, would *always* say their husband or wife was just exaggerating or trying to get an advantage in the custody case. As I evolved into a lawyer who focused on the true needs of the family and of the client, I would simply ask this question: "What's the worst thing you think your spouse will say about you?" The answer would often be something like, "Oh, she'll probably say I drink too much," or "He'll probably say I have a gambling problem."

From there it does not take much to get into a bit more realistic conversation about what's really going on in the lives of the parties. Again, I'm not saying your attorney should be doing anything to compromise your case here, but that it's appropriate to take a deeper look at some of the issues that will likely be raised in the case. I have had many clients who have admitted, "Yes, I can see why he/she is saying that." And in those cases it has allowed the attorneys to fashion agreements that allow the case to move forward and not fly off the rails. If there is a sticking point in your case, find a way to unstick it temporarily to move forward.

The most unconventional way to move forward is with a custody expert (most often a therapist or psychologist) who works with the clients outside of the presence of the lawyers to help the parties work through their custody issues. If you reach an arrangement your lawyers can write it up as a formal agreement and order of the court.

Most attorneys will not suggest this and many may caution against it if you suggest this as an option. There are valid legal reasons for your lawyer to do this. The main objection is that you will compromise your rights or agree to something that you otherwise would not agree to with legal counsel. If this may be true in your case, or if you are uncomfortable talking about a custody resolution without your attorney, then you should not pursue this as an option. If, however, you feel comfortable with what you think your family needs and you are able to have productive communication with your spouse in this type of setting, then you should pursue this option in your case. When my clients agree to this I always make myself available by phone and have them take a break and call me if they have any doubts. And, keep in mind, the agreement can always be made subject to attorney approval. With all these caveats, I have found third party mediation to be a much more efficient and cost effective way for clients to resolve their custody issues.

When using a third party to mediate your custody issues is just not appropriate, you will likely find yourself in a settlement facilitation with your lawyers and with another person, often another divorce lawyer, who will help the parties try to settle their case. Most often, all the other issues in your case that are still in dispute, along with your custody issues, will be part of this settlement process. As you have heard throughout this book, it is important to be clear about the outcomes that you want, but it is also important to understand that if you are to settle your case outside of court, then some compromise is required.

One common problem I see with settlement conferences is the use of "shuttle diplomacy." What happens in many cases is the attorney conducting the settlement proceeding will place the parties in separate rooms and move back and forth between the parties conveying offers to settle the case. This is a common practice in all types of legal cases. I understand why this happens, especially in divorce cases. The settlement facilitator (and very often the parties and their attorneys) are afraid to be in the same room because they believe there will be too much conflict between the parties and no progress will be made. That can certainly be true, but in most cases I have found that the close proximity of the parties, the ability to hear each side of the argument in the case, and to directly communicate, makes it much more likely for the parties to reach an agreement. It's fine if things get a little unpleasant. You have argued before, and the world did not come to an end. This is an emotional process and to deny that can often be detrimental to the case. If things do get out of control, however, you or your lawyer can call an end to the settlement proceedings.

When Court is Inevitable

Sometimes court is inevitable. If you have a spouse who is volatile, intractable, refuses to put the best interests of the child first, or is a threat to you or your child's safety, it's probably time to let your divorce assassin loose.

If a custody trial is in your future, many courts will appoint a psychologist or other mental health expert to make recommendations to the court. This is often done in the manner of a formal recommendation, but may take another form depending on your jurisdiction. This third party may be chosen by the parties or appointed by the court. He or she will be integral to whether you receive the custody arrangement you want, so take care in how you approach this process. If your lawyer is discussing the selection of this person with opposing counsel, he should be recommending someone who is most likely to side with your position. So, to the extent possible, your lawyer should know the expert's stances on things like: joint custody, a preference for men or women, their position on relocation, or the many other issues that might affect your custody case.

The custody evaluator will know nothing about you or your spouse except for the documents that you provide and the interviews she conducts. This is your opportunity to both "sell" yourself and cast a negative light (remember, now we are in divorce assassin mode) on your ex. The stakes are high at this point, so all negative information should be on the table and discussed with your attorney. This might include criminal records, domestic violence reports, work records (especially if they show poor performance or absence), medical records, and any unflattering texts/emails/Facebook posts and any other questionable communications. Sad but true: it is likely that the negative information you provide about your spouse will have more of an impact than the proof you offer to show you are a great parent.

Once the evaluator has completed her report and your court date has been set, it's time to get to work. Especially if the report includes elements that are not in your favor, *now* is your final chance to negotiate a deal before going before a judge. Even if you have to strike uncomfortable compromises with your ex, that is usually preferable to challenging the report in the courtroom. If you do end up in court arguing against any aspects of the expert's recommendation, make sure you and your attorney are ready to provide clear evidence to support your arguments.

Ideally, you will come to an acceptable custody arrangement without ever presenting your case to a judge. If not, I discuss courtroom strategies – for custody cases and other divorce scenarios – in more detail in Chapter 10.

The Takeaway

Whether six months old or a watchful teen, your divorce will be one of the defining moments of your child's life. The way in which it plays out will determine how well he or she adjusts to life after your divorce. How this will impact your child's life is up to you and your former spouse, with whom you will now and forever be co-parents. I encourage you to take the words in this chapter to heart, and to create a custody arrangement where your child has the best opportunity to thrive.

Chapter 9

Alimony

WHEN A LONG marriage comes to an end, there are several things divorce does not negate: years of shared history, children, and an obligation to be financially supportive to your spouse to the degree that it is both possible and necessary. This latter responsibility is where alimony (also known as spousal support) comes into play, and it has nothing to do with one party "taking the other for everything they're worth." Television and movies often portray alimony cases as a salacious process in which one party fights for an unfair advantage over the other. In reality, alimony is a legal acknowledgment of a partnership that, though legally ending, requires a certain level of financial responsibility from one spouse to the other.

Alimony, or spousal support, is commonly awarded when a couple has been married for a legally relevant period of time (which varies from state to state), and one spouse earns significantly more income than the other. The amount and duration of spousal support are either agreed to as part of your settlement or set by a judge. The modern concept of alimony originated from the English ecclesiastical courts which considered it the husband's duty to continue to support his wife since, in the eyes of God, divorce did not end the marriage. By the 19th century, alimony became a consequence of marital fault – if the husband was adulterous or abusive, he was still required to support his wife; if she was at fault, she forfeited her right to any alimony. With the rise of no-fault divorce, alimony has become more provisional, often awarded for a limited amount of time or not at all, depending on the circumstances of the case.

Alimony is subject to a variety of factors, not the least of which is the state in which you live. While alimony statutes exist in all states, the specifics can vary widely – in Utah, support cannot last longer than the marriage; in Georgia, adultery may preclude a spouse from receiving alimony. Some states are likely to award alimony if there was marital fault at play, while others tend to consider it a non-issue for a no-fault divorce.

That said, in general, alimony is calculated by considering the following factors:

- The length of the marriage;
- The lifestyle of the couple during the marriage;

- The dependent spouse's financial status;
- The dependent spouse's earning potential;
- The ability of the other party to pay.

These considerations will influence the nature of the support awarded. If there is a possibility that you will receive or be required to pay alimony, in one of your first meetings with your attorney she should explain to you the various types of alimony that might apply to your case. The following is a brief list of the different types of alimony that courts in the United States might award. Please remember that types of alimony vary greatly from state to state:

1) Rehabilitative Support

Rehabilitative support normally provides the receiving spouse with education, training, work experience, or other forms of rehabilitation that increase the receiving spouse's ability to earn income and become self-supporting. There is often a rehabilitation plan that the parties follow (like going to school), and there is normally a specific date that the support is to end.

2) Transitional Support

This type of support is meant to supplement one spouse's income for a limited period of time until he or she is able to transition into a more stable financial situation.

3) Long-term/Permanent Support

Usually granted after marriages of ten years of more, long-term support is granted if the dependent spouse is unlikely to re-enter the workforce in any significant way. It may end if the dependent spouse remarries or begins living with someone else, or if financial circumstances change significantly for either party.

4) Reimbursement Support

This type of alimony compensates the individual who forewent pursuing a career in lieu of supporting the spouse who trained for a lucrative professional path. With a divorce, the dependent spouse will not receive the anticipated benefits of her sacrifice, so this type of alimony attempts to seek fiscal balance.

Sometimes, alimony payments can be made modifiable or non-modifiable, paid in one lump sum, or structured in a number of other ways that can be beneficial to the parties. You should explore all of these options with your attorney.

Often, alimony payments are tax deductible for the paying spouse and must be reported as income by the recipient. This can be advantageous to both parties, as money is shifted from a higher tax bracket to a lower one. The tax savings that the higher earner receives can be a strong negotiating point when determining the amount of alimony set.

Why Alimony Exists in the First Place

"Why is alimony necessary?" Imagine this common scenario: one spouse (most commonly the wife if there are children in the picture – 29% of mothers in the U.S. do not work outside of the home[3]) quits working in her mid-twenties to stay home and raise the children. This was a choice the couple made together based on the idea that it would be better for one parent to act as the primary earner while the other raised the children and took care of the household needs. According to plan, the husband pushed his career forward with the goal of reaching a high level of financial compensation. The wife stayed at home and was instrumental in raising a beautiful family and helping the husband to succeed.

Now, with divorce on the horizon, the wife, who forestalled a meaningful career, must re-enter the workforce with little to no work experience, non-existent or vastly outdated education, and at an age that makes finding employment extremely difficult. In some cases, the spouse may have attained a certain age, or been away from the workforce for so long that the court will not require her to go back to work at all. In these types of cases, alimony is the only thing that stands between the wife and financial destitution.

An even more common scenario, is when one spouse requires financial support to get his or her life on track as a single person. In this situation, the

---

[3]Cohn, D'Vera; Gretchen Livingston; and Wendy Wang. "After Decades of Decline, A Rise in Stay-at-Home Mothers" Pew Research, 4/8/14. http://www.pewsocialtrends.org/2014/04/08/after-decades-of-decline-a-rise-in-stay-at-home-mothers/#fn-18853-5

parties agree to, or the court awards, alimony for a specified amount of time. This is what you do not see in the media. What you do see on TV is the much less frequent scenario in which the couple has achieved a very high level of income and lifestyle and the court may award alimony in an amount that allows the non-earning spouse to continue his or her lifestyle in the manner to which he or she was accustomed.

People get married because they love each other. At least that's what they tell each other and that's what they often pledge to each other in some form of official ceremony. But once it's over, it's as if none of this had ever happened. In initial divorce consultations, I am often shocked to hear how one spouse talks about the other, and to listen to the total disregard that a husband or wife has for the financial well-being of the person he or she once loved.

Divorce clients tend to overcomplicate the question of alimony, attaching all sorts of emotional baggage to it. In fact, from a purely legal standpoint, calculating a reasonable amount of alimony is not rocket science. It is tied very closely to the parties' incomes (or potential incomes) and budgets. Most often, there is a predictable range within which alimony is likely to fall, a figure that can be tossed back and forth between lawyers that know the income and budgets that are available, your state's guidelines, and the judge's tendencies if you end up in trial. Reaching an equitable agreement should be well within the range of any competent, client-focused attorneys ... except when it's not.

Bob and Sarah were married for 10 years and had two children together. Their settlement negotiations had been proceeding smoothly; both seemed eager to get on with their lives. The remaining snag was the amount of alimony Sarah would be granted: both had agreed to a duration of five years so Sarah could receive support while she became more established in her field, but they were $500 apart. Based upon her budget, Sarah requested $1,000 per month in alimony. For his own reasons, Bob had set his maximum payment at $500 per month.

Negotiations were at a standstill. Bob told his lawyer that if Sarah would not adjust her demand that he would happily go to trial. While her lawyer advised her against compromising her position, Sarah made a last-ditch concession: she would agree to $750 per month. Rather than meet her halfway, Bob convinced himself that he wanted his day in court. He believed his reasons for sticking to his number were sound. Wouldn't it be satisfying if the judge backed him up? And anyway, he had heard the judge in his case was rather conservative with alimony awards. He'd take his chances.

Bob and Sarah had found themselves at the most treacherous fork on the road to divorce: settle or go to trial. At this juncture you *must* keep yourself focused on the bottom line of your case. Do not blindly rely on your attorney. Believe me, your attorney is competitive and wants to "win" your case just as badly (and maybe even more) as you do. Using Bob's and Sarah's case, let me present two scenarios to illustrate just how much it actually costs to "win" your alimony case.

Scenario #1: Bob agrees to pay Sarah $750 per month. With the case settled, Sarah's attorney agreed to prepare all remaining legal documents and Bob incurred no additional attorney fees. A week passed, the documents were signed and filed, and everyone was satisfied. Bob and Sarah remained friends and were determined to be thoughtful co-parents to their two small children. Although the extra cost of paying Sarah $750 rather than the $500 he had in mind would be $15,000 over five years, because of Bob's tax bracket (30%), the actual cost of the alimony was $10,000.

Scenario #2: Bob and Sarah head to court. It took them eight months to get a trial date. Meanwhile, Bob was required to pay Sarah interim support of $400 per month. Sarah was deeply resentful that Bob was forcing them to drag this out. She was not looking to cash in, she just needed to be able to afford the basics: the mortgage on the house that she lived in with the kids, the car, vet bills for the dog, utilities, etc.

Their court date finally arrived. After a two-day trial, the judge agreed with Bob that Sarah should receive $500 per month. Bob was elated at this victory

... until he met with his accountant. The final bill for his court costs and attorney fees came to $14,000. Add to this the $3,200 he paid Sarah in interim support, and his "day in court" cost him over $17,200. Essentially, he paid his lawyer what he could have paid Sarah, who now hated his guts, and he lost more money in interim support and lost wages.

Let's have a look at the two financial scenarios side by side:

BOB COMPROMISES	BOB GOES TO TRIAL AND "WINS"
Extra alimony payments based on compromise at settlement: $15,000	Extra alimony payments based on compromise at settlement: $0
Attorney fees after settlement conference: $0	Attorney fees after settlement conference: $14,000
Interim support awaiting trial after settlement: $0	Interim support awaiting trial after settlement: $3,200
Total additional costs and attorney's fees based on compromise agreement: $15,000	Total additional costs and attorney's fees based on going to trial: $17, 200

On the chart above, I did not list the value of a healthy, ongoing relationship with your former spouse, and I would never try to put a monetary value on successfully co-parenting your children. But I will tell you that, unfortunately, many divorce and family law firms make a large percentage of their profits on post-divorce litigation. For the sake of your entire family, put emotion aside and focus on the bottom line of your alimony case.

Alimony: Not Just for the Jet Set

Alimony has become something of a dirty word in our culture. It brings forth images of bejeweled women living large while their ex-husbands fork over half their earnings. Celebrities and business moguls may dominate headlines, but divorce is not relegated to the 1 percent. It happens to couples who make $50,000 a year with little hope for advancement, and it is in the middle- and lower-class families that alimony becomes such a devastating issue.

In lower- and middle-class families (and even in some upper-middle-class families), there can be little debate that a dependent spouse needs alimony just to live. But as the saying goes, you can't get water from a stone; if there's no money to give, alimony is a non-starter. Take Sean and Sandy, a restaurant manager making $55,000 and an office assistant making $20,000, respectively. In addition to car payments, they had amassed a significant amount of credit card debt. Out of the gate, Sean offered to pay child support according to statute, as well as take on most of the credit card debt (though he was only required to pay half). He knew Sandy would have a hard time, given her limited earnings.

Even though Sandy's lawyer was well aware of this, he insisted on a high amount of alimony. In settlement facilitation, Sean offered a small amount of alimony, even though it was inappropriate. Unwavering, Sandy's team forced the divorce proceedings into court where a judge awarded no alimony and split the credit card debt equally between the parties. Both parties now had enormous legal fees to pay, further exacerbating their financial straits.

There are two key lessons to be gleaned from Sean and Sandy's situation. First, if you do end up going to trial, know that all of the agreements you made in good faith beforehand (like Sean's offer to pay the majority of the credit card debt) no longer apply. For a judge, only the facts of divorce are salient – not the bargains you've made between one another since separating. Second, although one spouse may *need* alimony, there is another crucial part of the equation that many people simply ignore: the other party's *ability to pay*. And this is why divorce is so often financially ruinous for low-income earners, especially when children are in the picture: where you once pooled your income and shared the expenses, now the expenses remain while your income may dip precipitously.

Chasing money that isn't there only leads to disappointment and a jaw-dropping bill from your lawyer. Fortunately, there are creative alternatives that can help balance the scales. I advise my clients in this situation to look for community assets that can be traded for spousal support. Retirement accounts and pensions are often split evenly between parties, so if you are a dependent spouse, one solution would be to ask for an unequal distribution of retirement assets (in your favor) in exchange for waiving alimony.

Another option is equity in the home. Often, it is very advantageous for the non- earning spouse to be able to remain in the marital home, and if there is a large amount of equity in the home, this can be traded against alimony. Remember that alimony is usually taxable to the recipient, but receiving a larger part of your home's equity as part of your divorce settlement is probably not subject to taxation.

For people with higher incomes the same rules still apply. Couples who are flying high together and enjoying a comfortable lifestyle during their marriage will often face financial challenges when divorcing. People in this situation must pay special attention to the attorneys they hire. Unfortunately, some lawyers look at clients with a lot of disposable income as little more than a big legal fee. So when you do pick a lawyer, be very clear about the outcomes you want before you pay that big retainer.

Finding Your Alimony Number

Rich, poor, or somewhere in the middle, if yours is an alimony case, how do you decide a fair amount to request or to pay in alimony? Too often, my clients, women especially, underestimate what they actually need to live. Rather than running through a realistic budget they simply throw out a number they hope is "fair." Or, emotions and fear cloud financial realities: "I don't want *anything* from him!" or "He said I would never see a dime and I can't handle fighting with him." It can be incredibly difficult to be in the position of asking for money from someone with whom you have a contentious relationship. And though these feelings are understandable, you hired a lawyer for a reason – as an advocate, someone to fight for you when you're not ready or capable to fight. Though it may be uncomfortable now, remember that you have only one chance to settle your divorce, and when it's over it will be solely up to you to provide for yourself.

My client Carol is a good example of someone who undervalued what she would really need post-divorce. In our initial consultation, she told me she and her husband had already agreed to the terms of their divorce. He was going to pay her $400 per month in alimony, and she wanted to know if I thought this was fair. (She assured me her husband was a very fair guy). I took out my trusty master budget and began running through it with her: haircuts and colors, gas, car insurance, utilities, the list went on and on until "fair" started to look very different from $400 per month.

I then took a quick look at their tax returns. Carol's husband Bill owned his own business. I asked a few questions about how certain expenses were paid: dinners, new computers for the home, cell phone bills, and most often the answer was that the company paid for it. It turns out his actual income was much higher than the tax return indicated. After hearing this, Carol hired me to negotiate a pre-filing settlement. The result: her husband agreed to pay $1,500 per month in alimony (and I think he got off easy!). Carol understood what she really needed after putting together an accurate budget, and that was what helped to resolve her case. We did not need to go through a lengthy, expensive divorce. Her husband was a businessman who understood the numbers, and he hired a lawyer who carried out his wishes, to settle the divorce without destroying their finances. It was just that Bill's idea and Carol's idea of "fair" were very different until they looked at the real numbers.

Getting to a reasonable alimony figure requires determining your post-divorce budget. This is an exercise few people enjoy, but it is crucial information and a key negotiating tool. **I have created a free master budget tool you can download at: www.DivorceDeclassified.com/budget**.

It also means arming yourself with knowledge (about your expenditures, your income, your spouse's income, retirement accounts, and other assets) and discussing these facts with your lawyer early on in the process.

Keep in mind, there are lawyers who will be happy to do you the disservice of billing your retainer by fighting over every little piece of information and making unnecessary discovery requests. If money is a concern for you, it is in your power to curtail unnecessary back-and-forth between your lawyer and opposing counsel. Begin the process knowing the range of alimony you need, armed with the information to prove your case. Conserve money by asking for an early settlement with the goal of wrapping up this difficult period of your life in as short a time period as possible.

One strategy for staying out of court is settling your case early by compromising on a fair alimony amount. For both parties it is important to understand how the courts in your state handle income and debt while your case is pending. Most states will divide your income and debt in some fashion until your case is over. Often this is called interim support. You must be aware of this because it can create a lot of leverage for the person requesting alimony. Many times, the interim payment may be much higher than the amount of alimony a court would award. This allows the requesting spouse to drag the case out and collect interim payments while negotiating a higher alimony award. This scenario doesn't mean a paying spouse should roll over and pay any amount, but as discussed earlier, things like ongoing attorney's fees, interim support payments, and other costs should be considered when settling an alimony case.

An Alimony Checklist

How do you know if the facts of your case support an award of alimony? What type of alimony will you likely pay/be awarded? Below is a brief alimony checklist to help you get started.

Is your case an alimony case? If so, you must be able to answer 'yes' to the following three questions:

1) Was your marriage long enough to qualify? (this is not an easy answer and you may need to do research or get a definitive answer to this in a consultation)
2) Is there a need for alimony? and
3) Is there an ability to pay by the other party?

If you do have an alimony case, how does your state calculate alimony? If there is a formula, plug in your information to get an idea of where you are headed. If there's not a formula, what are the other factors (length of marriage, lifestyle, etc.) the courts look at in your area? Every state weighs these factors differently, so do your research or get these answers in your consultation.

What is your BATNA (Best Alternative to a Negotiated Agreement)? You should definitely know the maximum alimony award a court in your jurisdiction is likely to award in your case. If your lawyer balks at giving you a number, ask them to give you a number he or she is confident the court would never exceed. That is your BATNA.

Alimony exists for a reason, and the reason is this: when you choose to marry and build a life with someone, that promise has a ripple effect that can last long after you've divorced.

In scenarios of disparate income between spouses, alimony is a way to acknowledge responsibility for our choices and respect for one another. Ironically, the subject of alimony too often tends to elicit the opposite sentiments. Whether you are a dependent or supporting spouse, good communication with your lawyer, solid facts, and a dispassionate attitude will be key tools for achieving a satisfactory resolution.

Chapter 10

The Day You Walk into Court

IN A PERFECT world, the dissolution of your marriage would never be played out in a courtroom. For various reasons we have already discussed, working out the details of your divorce *without* the direct involvement of a judge is almost always preferable. That said, family court exists for a reason – there are some cases that absolutely demand judicial intervention. If you find yourself heading down this path, there is likely something of extreme importance to you (usually kids and/or alimony) hanging in the balance. Given the gravity of what is at stake, understanding courtroom protocol, preparing for how to comport yourself, and knowing what to expect from both your lawyer and the judge could not be more critical.

The court functions as a legal foundation for your divorce. It gives the process a necessary structure, even if you never set foot in a courtroom. Your lawyer may file a multitude of motions regarding division of debt, custody arrangements, temporary support, etc. These motions are then placed on the court's docket, meaning a date is set for the issue to be heard by a judge. More often than not, the details are worked out between lawyers before the motion's hearing date, and it is then taken off the docket. In this way, a divorce case moves forward until all the issues are agreed upon. It is not unusual, however, to have a number of small hearings regarding motions that have been filed in your case. These hearings are used to resolve what are considered "pre-trial" issues, disagreements that require the court's intervention, but are not part of the larger settlement of the case.

But when all pre-trial motions have been resolved and there are still significant issues in your case that cannot be resolved; when you've exhausted all other options and cannot reach a reasonable compromise; when you are truly, irrevocably stuck on opposing sides of major issues, your case will proceed to trial.

The key here is being absolutely sure that the disagreement(s) at hand merit the cost, time, and uncertainty of going to trial. What exactly is it that's holding back resolution? Ask your lawyer to explain exactly why you are going to trial, because you're about to rack up a hefty legal bill. Again, this is not to say a trial is not necessary (lawyers hate going to trial, by the way, because it's a HUGE amount of work), it's just that you should be very clear why you are agreeing to take this step. Too often, people end up in trial because they really do not understand their worst and best case scenarios or because their lawyer did a lousy job handling their cases before the trial setting.

When you decide that trial is appropriate for your case, it is crucial to thoroughly understand all possible outcomes. Going before a judge involves surrendering control over the results of your case. Your fate will now be in the hands of someone who will only know you for a few hours and will receive half of what she knows about you from your opposition.

Often, a judge will not rule on your case until a significant time after you trial has taken place. This is not like a criminal case, where the jury decides your guilt or innocence before you leave court. Most divorce courts have very large dockets and it may take weeks before the judge issues her ruling. Be fully aware of the possible consequences of whatever is decided, including the timing of when the ruling goes into effect. If it's a financial issue, how will you handle your money going forward? If you have to move out of the family home, where will you live? If your custody arrangement is changing, how will you prepare for that?

I emphasize an aggressive pursuit of specificity with your legal counsel because I have seen many, many lawyers and their clients sitting in court not really knowing why they are there or asking for something that is utterly nonsensical. Without a proper conversation regarding the merits of their cases, clueless, unprepared lawyers and their deer-in-headlights clients waste everyone's time and money. You want to ask the judge to take the kid away from your stay-at-home ex-wife? You better have a damn good reason for making that argument. You want your spouse to pay a huge amount of alimony? You better have a solid budget and proof your spouse can afford it.

Here's what I tell my clients: "Let's give it the 'Say it with a straight face test.'" Say the thing you want out loud and imagine yourself in front of a judge who has never seen you before, who has no knowledge of you or your spouse, and see if you can actually ask for it without making a weird face. If the client says yes, I then take on the role of the judge and ask a few of the toughest questions the judge will likely ask. This is not to say your lawyer should not pursue certain legal issues that may be challenging. Ask for what you want, but remain sensible to the realities of what you are likely to get.

The Television Trap

Television and movies have made us all feel well-acquainted with the courtroom setting. And, truly, it does look the same as it does on TV. But when it's your day in court, it won't *feel* the same. It can be scary; you'll be nervous. In an effort to dispel some of the uncertainty, let's run through what to expect and how you should comport yourself on the day you go to court.

Before you even leave the house, your choices matter. Though it may sound cliché, dressing nicely can make all the difference when you appear before a judge. Think about it: this person has very little information or time in order to make an accurate assessment of your character. Your choice of dress is a key part of this process; you want to show the court respect. For men, wear a suit if you have one. If not, don't go out and acquire something cheap and ill-fitting – if you're a guy who doesn't normally wear a suit and looks uncomfortable, it can come off as contrived. Instead, choose a nice shirt and slacks. That look is perfectly acceptable and I often recommend it over something more formal to a lot of my clients. For women, conservative is normally the way to go: a well-tailored dress or suit, or a nice blouse and dress pants.

For all clients, male or female, if you are unsure how a judge might view something, cover it up or don't wear it. This includes tattoos, jewelry, piercings, tight-fitting clothing, unusual hairstyles, and every other personal style piece you can imagine. This is not your moment for personal expression – it's about fitting into societal "norms." And any lawyer who's not telling you the same thing isn't doing his or her job.

Now you're on your way. Keep in mind that it takes time to get to court, especially considering the court-house may be an unfamiliar destination for you. Give yourself plenty of leeway here – you do not want the added stress of rushing and you do NOT want to be late. Between finding parking, the line into court, and especially going through security, locating your ap-pointed courtroom may take you twice as long as you think. Plan on it. Calm down. Get there on time.

As you enter the courtroom, your team and your spouse's team may be the only people in attendance, but probably not. Often judges will take multiple hearings, one after the next. If this is the case, you will be required to wait in the seating area until your case is called. Typically, there will be gates separating this area from where the court proper starts, which includes one of two counsel tables where you will sit with your lawyer, facing the judge. The table will have a microphone on it. Note: the mic picks up every whisper, sneeze, and cough. If you want to say something to your lawyer privately, be sure to cover it or hit the mute button.

Who else will be there? The judge, obviously. If he or she isn't already on the bench when you settle in, be sure to stand when the judge enters the room (and also when he or she exits). Besides the parties relevant to your case, there will be other various court personnel in attendance: a court reporter who will take down everything that is said, a clerk who handles administration for the judge, and a bailiff who handles security and may hand evidence back and forth to the bench.

At the risk of stating the obvious, as your trial or hearing commences, stay in control of yourself. No matter what happens – your ex lies, his lawyer is not a nice guy, you don't like the judge – maintain a respectful comportment. I say this because time and again I've seen people completely derail their cases by rolling their eyes, loudly sighing, chewing gum, or being otherwise obnoxious. In my own cases, I have had the most normal of clients do something that simply takes my breath away. I once had a male client laugh when opposing counsel talked about required medical treatment for the client's daughter. I once had a female client yell to opposing counsel that she hoped the lawyer could never conceive children (and the court reporter got that on the record). Even the best clients lose their cool.

In a way, this is understandable: the combination of anxiety and fear of authority is a muddy mix that can bring out the surly teen in all of us. You must be aware of this in advance and resolve to keep it in check.

Once the judge begins to hear your case, it's time for your lawyer to take center stage and hopefully shine. Now, before you ever get to this point you hopefully have already evaluated how your attorney performs in court. If your case is going to trial it is very likely that you have already been to court on one or more pre-trial issues. In every instance in which your lawyer appears in court, carefully analyze her performance. Watch closely: Is she making your voice heard? Is she organized? Prepared? Is she an effective communicator? Does she handle objections well? Does the judge know her? Does she seem credible? Does the judge listen to her arguments with respect and due consideration?

Representation in the normal course of your case is one thing (and many lawyers are good at this), but representation in court and especially in trial is a completely different thing. If you feel that your lawyer is not effective in court, consider a change in legal counsel as soon as possible. This is different than simply not getting the result you want. Rather, it's discovering that your lawyer – who may be perfectly charming and professional in an office setting – simply can't get the job done in court. This is not uncommon among divorce attorneys, who rarely have to perform in a courtroom setting (only 5-10% of divorce cases actually go to trial[4]).

How to Testify

As part of your preparation for going to trial, you and your lawyer should have discussed the possibility of you having to testify. In a full-on trial, you will surely be called on to testify before the judge, and in some jurisdictions, a jury. At hearings on motions, many times the judge will just hear from the lawyers, but sometimes the court will want to hear testimony from the parties as well. If testifying is *at all* possible, you must be fully prepared for what questions your attorney will ask you, what the judge might ask you, and what opposing counsel is likely to ask.

Testifying in court can be intimidating, to say the least. At the very least, I *always* role play the questions I intend to ask my client. The words you use, how you act when you respond to questions, and how you carry yourself can have a HUGE impact on how the judge receives your testimony.

In addition, I also grill my client with the most likely questions opposing counsel will ask. This is *not* complicated. Any decent attorney knows almost exactly what opposing counsel is going to ask, and where your case is vulnerable. If your attorney cannot

---

[4] Anton, Leonora LaPeter. "The divorce from hell, the battle for alimony and emptied pockets" Tampa Bay Times, 4/3/13.

quickly point out the problems with your case, you have hired the wrong attorney.

As you prepare, keep in mind the three most important points when testifying in court: (1) On cross-examination, answer only the question that is asked. Many clients offer more information than the question requires, and almost always this information hurts their cases; (2) If your attorney objects to a question, stop talking and wait for the judge to rule. I have seen many parties answer a question in the middle of the judge ruling that the question should not be answered; (3) Make at least some eye contact with the judge, or the jury if you happen to have one.

There is a trend in family courts toward informality and the possibility that the judge can get just a bit off track. You may be in front of the judge to address temporary spousal support when the opposing counsel ambushes you with last weekend's party pictures on Facebook. The judge may pounce on this opportunity to take a more comprehensive look at you and your family. And while you and your lawyer were well-prepared to answer financial questions, now you're on the spot about things that are completely unrelated to your hearing. My point here: when you go to court, you are opening your life up for scrutiny. There is no law preventing the judge from asking you all kinds of uncomfortable questions that you must answer truthfully.

You may feel exposed and upset as the judge attempts to uncover the inner workings of your family life. But take a moment to put yourself in the position of the judge: here is a person whom you're asking to make HUGE decisions about your family. You may be asking the judge to decide who should have primary custody of your child. You may be asking the judge to decide how much alimony should be paid in your case. These are life-altering decisions.

The judge does not know you. She has no idea what kind of person you are, what kind of intentions you have, whether you are a good parent, or what might necessarily be fair in your case. She gets only the limited information you and your attorney provide to her. She may have literally thousands of cases on her docket. She may have read your pleadings, or she may not have read them at all. She may be in a good mood or a bad mood on the day of your trial.

Ask yourself: how would I view my case if I knew nothing about me? Often, when I sit down with clients and ask them how they would rule on a case, knowing virtually nothing about either party, they get a sobering view of how their case might be resolved.

The Takeaway

Family court is an imperfect system at best. Not because the court is flawed, but because families really have no business being in court at all. Most often, clients spend the time, the energy, and the great outpouring of money that going to court demands – and the result is not a "win" for either side. There's no victory to be found here. In fact, at the end of the day, most couples wind up with less than what they originally hoped for or would have gotten had they settled: less money, less control, less flexibility with custody arrangements, and certainly less of an amicable relationship going forward.

There is most definitely a better option than a divorce trial. The next chapter will lead you out of this gloomy place and into the light of divorce mediation and what I hope will be the future of divorce in this country.

Chapter 11

The Holy Grail of Divorce Resolutions

Y OU CANNOT SHAKE hands with a clenched fist.
– *Indira Gandhi*

As we have seen, there are countless missteps that can turn the unfortunate circumstance of your divorce into a true nightmare. But this is in no way inevitable. The absolute best way to avoid these treacherous waters is divorce mediation, a non-adversarial approach that allows you to take control of the separation process. If you are a good candidate for mediation, this route can save you time, big money, and plenty of heartache.

So what, exactly, is divorce mediation? Mediation is the process by which an impartial professional helps you and your spouse resolve your differences in an atmosphere of mutual respect. The goal of mediation is a mutually agreed-upon, legally-binding resolution of all of the issues in your divorce case. This agreement is reached through a series of orderly steps that include productive communication and information gathering. Rather than letting two lawyers trained to fight turn your case into a bloodbath, or placing your family's future at the mercy of the court, mediation allows you to remain in complete control of the outcome.

Seeking out mediation requires a willingness to veer away from the typical blunt force trauma of divorce. Because here's the truth: most lawyers can't or won't deliver mediation as one of their services. Mediation generates less revenue, demands more creativity, and requires interpersonal skills most lawyers do not possess. Lawyers educated in adversarial tactics are often skeptical about the process and few have formal training in this area. Mediation is a relatively new approach to divorce in this country, and some lawyers think it is unethical because a lawyer cannot represent two clients with opposing interests. But here's the thing: You are not asking your lawyer to act as a lawyer. The lawyer is functioning as a mediator, and the fee agreement you sign should reflect that. The lawyer is NOT representing either one of you; he or she is guiding you through a specific process.

Mediation is certainly not appropriate in every case, especially if you have difficult issues for which you feel you need representation. But mediation should *always* at least be considered. A skilled divorce mediator can often resolve a case that you might feel is hopeless.

This distrust, on the part of both the clients and their lawyers, was apparent in a recent case that came through New Mexico Legal Group. George and his wife Jane sought out our firm specifically for divorce mediation, as we employ lawyers trained in this practice. After a long marriage, they had arrived at different places in their lives. George still presided over his successful accounting firm, while Jane had retired and was doing volunteer work abroad. Their kids were grown, so custody wasn't an issue. But there was the business to deal with, two homes, retirement accounts, and a *long* marriage

Jane and George had their disagreements, but both sincerely wanted the best for one another. At my firm, we normally charge a flat fee for mediation services, which includes a fixed number of mediation sessions. These parties had a very large estate and some complicated financial issues, so our attorney quoted a flat fee that was in line with what the case required. Once the parties both signed the initial agreement, things proceeded smoothly – their first mediation session covered a lot of ground, and both George and Jane were on task for providing the necessary documents and other materials. Only a few outstanding differences remained, and our attorney was pleased that this case – which could have been complex and lengthy given the size of the estate – was being resolved efficiently and amicably.

That is, until the attorney was required to send over the paperwork to both George's and Jane's *other* lawyers. Each had hired an additional set of attorneys at "prominent" local firms to look over our work, at significant cost. It is sad to say, but George paid twice the amount of legal fees to his back-up counsel that we charged to resolve the entire case. Jane paid one-and-a-half times our fee. The result: neither party agreed with any of these superfluous lawyers' make-work suggestions. Of course, it was this couple's prerogative to hire outside counsel for a second opinion if that made them comfortable. But the whole purpose of mediation is to streamline the process, saving everyone time and money. Paying over 200% more in legal fees defeated this purpose. Mediation can seem too good to be true. But honestly, that's only because the "normal" divorce process is so toxic that *anything* seems like a better alternative.

This case illustrates the challenge that the perception of divorce mediation faces. Is it real? Is it legally binding? Is it for wimps? I'm here to tell you it's the one process that can completely transform our broken divorce system.

How to Find a Mediator

So you want to seek out a mediated divorce? Where do you start? The first step in this process is hiring a divorce mediator who is right for you. While many mediators are not attorneys, I recommend finding an experienced divorce lawyer who has had mediation training. I have seen many skilled mediators without a law degree make crucial mistakes when settling a case. As well, a mediator with deep knowledge of how divorce works in your state is often better positioned to suggest options in the context of the law. She can utilize her expertise to help you craft a workable and enforceable resolution. In many mediation cases, the lawyer will be able to inform clients how the court would most likely rule on a particular legal issue. This also gives the clients reassurance that they are doing the right thing by avoiding court.

The best first step is to go online and seek out firms that advertise divorce mediation as part of their practice. When you make that initial call and say you are seeking a consultation for a mediated divorce, the staff's response should be immediate recognition of what you are talking about and to whom to direct your request. Beware of the receptionist who does not seem familiar with mediation as a concept. "You're interested in what?" or "Let me put you on hold and see if we do that," are red flags that mean this firm may be happy to take you on as a client, but will likely not have the expertise you are seeking.

Once you have settled upon a good candidate, you and your spouse will attend an initial consultation. This should always be done together. From the mediator's perspective, she will be determining whether your case is appropriate for mediation. In some cases, especially where there seems to be a large power imbalance between the parties, and definitely if it seems one party is forcing the other into mediation, the lawyer may decline to take your case. But usually, if you are there together asking about mediation, the attorney will agree to mediate your case. Initial questions from the mediator will likely touch upon any potential hot buttons: complex legal issues, how far apart you are in terms of custody and alimony, and – importantly – how you communicate.

What should you be looking for in this first meeting? A good divorce mediator will have engaged in a significant amount of training in this specialty and will be able to tell you about it if you ask. This is not always necessary, however. Some attorneys have been practicing so long and have been involved in so many cases that they instinctively know how to mediate cases. This can work, but they should still have actual experience acting as a mediator. Your mediator should also be a good communicator and that should be obvious from the start. She should listen to both you and your spouse equally. Another key to mediation is creativity – an effective mediator will be open to ideas and have enough command of the situation to suggest her own thoughts when agreements are stalled.

Once you decide to move forward with your divorce mediator, she will suggest a payment structure that will be reflected in a fee agreement you will both sign. This often lays out a certain set number of mediation sessions. In my experience, if a couple needs more than two or three half-day mediation sessions, it is unlikely they will be able to settle their case in this manner. There are certainly exceptions, however, and as long as couples are making progress, I will continue to mediate the case, regardless of the number of sessions needed.

After your first meeting, it will be your job to go home and gather the relevant documents and information for your case: property/debt lists, home valuations, proposed custody schedules, etc. Remember: mediation means you don't have lawyers going back and forth with discovery requests, asking for often unnecessary information that can take months to produce. This is one of the ways mediation simplifies matters. You are responsible for doing your own homework, for procuring the information you need to come to an agreement.

Once your mediation sessions begin in earnest, there are several steps that typically take place: a) additional information is gathered based upon the issues that arise during these sessions; b) brainstorming the issues at hand, which includes the mediator identifying all possible options without judgment; c) negotiating and ultimately making the necessary compromises to come to a resolution; d) writing up/signing the agreement.

Sounds simple enough, right? Yes and no. Divorce mediation is a highly productive process, but it can also be incredibly intense. You'll be sitting in the same room with your spouse and the (hopefully) experienced mediator, hashing over the issues that are most dear to your heart and your future. Mediation gives you the opportunity to be heard in a positive, supportive environment that focuses on the future rather than the past. But these sessions can be awfully emotional, which is why hiring a skillful mediator is so crucial.

Imagine you're trying to solve the puzzle of your custody arrangement. It's so easy – so human – to get sidetracked by resentment and who-did-what-to-whom. But a great mediator steps in and calmly reframes the arguments. A great mediator is the impartial voice of reason who keeps you on track and encourages each of you to bring your best self to the process. This can be especially beneficial in cases where there are custody disagreements. The focus on non-adversarial communication eases tensions that children so easily pick up on, imagining and fearing the worst. And, mediated child support agreements result in 80% voluntary compliance, versus a mere 40% for litigated arrangements[5].

Both parties almost always attend mediation sessions, but there are some circumstances where it can be helpful for one or both of you to meet with the mediator individually. This can happen if progress has stalled and the mediator needs to get to the bottom of one party's *need*, which can be difficult to state in front of the other party, rather than their *position*. It does not imply favoritism, but rather gives the mediator the opportunity to hear what each spouse is saying clearly. This almost always happens during a joint mediation session, where the mediator takes a break and talks to one or both of the parties separately.

When the mediation is over, and all outstanding issues have been negotiated, you and your spouse will both sign a summary of your agreement. The mediator (this can only happen if your mediator is an attorney) will then take these provisions and turn them into more detailed, formal divorce documents that will be filed with the court. At this point, you've avoided the time consuming back-and-forth of lawyers (not to mention exorbitant legal fees), and/or the waiting game of getting a court date. With time and money in

---

[5]Karlsson, Rackham. "Choosing Divorce Mediation Through Statistical Analysis" Zephyr Legal Services, 1/9/14.
http://www.zephyrlaw.com/family-law-blog/bid/366619/Choosing-Divorce-Mediation-Through-Statistical-Analysis

your pocket, you can take a deep breath and move on with your life.

The Best Candidates for Divorce Mediation

Divorce mediation works best for people who don't hate each other, and who want to try to preserve their relationship as friends and/or parents. Imagine a couple with limited resources that would otherwise simply file an uncontested divorce but have a significant difference of opinion on the custody arrangement. Mediation is a good option for them.

Or, take a high asset couple who want to avoid predatory law firms who tend to view the wealthy as a huge payday. Mediation allows them to take their time and settle their case in a way that preserves their finances and relationships.

Mediation is also a great option for a low-income family with serious debt issues. They may have no money for lawyers but need an expert to walk them through how to share debt and avoid bankruptcy (or perhaps file a joint bankruptcy). In all of these scenarios, there is an honest desire for cooperation combined with the need for a neutral counselor to help them resolve their legal issues.

Those who seek out this path tend to settle successfully, but if a mutual agreement cannot be found, the parties must retain new lawyers and begin at the beginning, forfeiting the money already spent on the failed mediation. Certainly, mediation is not the best option for everyone. As we have already seen, cases involving domestic violence, cases with great power imbalances, and cases in which the parties cannot communicate, may not be appropriate cases for mediation. So think about these three negative scenarios – do they apply to your case? If not, you should definitely be considering mediation.

Below is a brief outline of the advantages and disadvantages of using mediation for your divorce:

Advantages

- You take complete control of your case.
- You pick a lawyer with whom you are both comfortable. (And this person usually tends to be a good communicator given his or her interest/training in mediation.)
- You control the pace of the proceedings, which means mediation is usually much quicker than a typical divorce.
- You save money.
- You avoid going to court.
- It's less traumatic for your children.
- You sidestep having to take aggressive adversarial positions.
- You preserve your relationship.
- You retain your confidentiality.

Disadvantages

- If you do not settle, you have spent money you cannot get back.
- If you do not settle, you will have to find new attorneys and your case will be back to square one.
- Not possible in cases of abuse, huge power imbalances, or lack of communication.
- Requires a fairly high level of communication and civility.
- Can be hard to find a qualified mediator

Some Interesting Statistics

There are approximately 2,400 divorces per day in the U.S. For those for whom mediation is a viable option, it is the *only* rational choice. Start to finish, an average mediation can cost as little as $5,000, compared to the $20,000 you would likely pay, *per person*, to have even a simple divorce litigated. Additionally, the average time involved in mediation is three to six months, compared to two years for a case that goes to trial[6]. That said, most people are unaware that this dignified path to separation is even an option.

This lack of information pertaining to mediation is due in part to a failure within the legal community to

[6]National Conflict Resolution Center." Getting Divorced: Two Ways To Go About It."
http://www.ncrconline.com/Divorce/MediationVsLitigation.php

embrace divorce mediation, preferring instead to preserve the status quo that drains people's time, money, and peace of mind. It's really no surprise. Mediation is hard work: it demands a high level of legal and social skill that many attorneys simply do not possess. This is why, when you walk into a divorce lawyer's office for the first time, you'll likely be steered toward an adversarial approach: "Here's what I can *get* for *you*."

In part, the traditional path to litigation is based on fear. Clients think they can't get a good deal if they don't fight for it. Lawyers fear that if everyone mediated their cases they would lose significant income for their law practices. The reality is, many couples will still not be able to mediate their divorce cases, for reasons ranging from feelings hurt beyond repair to complex legal issues that require lawyers for both parties. Lawyers should never be afraid to get mediation training and offer it as part of their services.

Even given the clear advantages of mediation, out of the thousands of couples who divorce each year, there is only a small portion who currently seek it out. Though the resources exist in most cities across the country, the culture of adversarial divorce tends to outshine mediation's more subtle light. There are so many couples who would benefit from this solution – and they just don't know it's an option. I sincerely hope to change that fact.

Chapter 12

The Good Divorce

I N THE PROCESS of letting go, you will lose many
things from the past, but you will find yourself.
- *Deepak Chopra*

What do you want out of your divorce? A stable
financial future? Happy, well-adjusted kids? A fresh
shot at love? Perhaps you'd simply like it to be behind
you. I ask these questions because I have seen too
many people enter this process without a clear
outcome – disempowered men and women who throw
their hands in the air, surrendering their authority to
their lawyers and the siren call of damaging emotions.

That you are *not* in control of your divorce is a
grand illusion. My hope is that the lessons found
within these pages have helped pull back the curtain
to reveal the "Great Oz" of divorce for what it really is:
a system that promotes acrimony rather than

harmony. Now that you know this, you have the power to approach your divorce differently, to be good to both yourself and your family. This may or may not mean exploring mediation as a viable option. At the very least, it signifies approaching this difficult time with maturity, self-knowledge, and a willingness to communicate thoughtfully. For even if you and your spouse are far apart on the tough issues of alimony and child custody, these are the skills that will help you inch closer to resolution without tearing your family to pieces.

If you reach the other side of your divorce with your family's well-being and peace of mind intact, you have won; you have experienced what I call a 'good' divorce. A good divorce means everyone is still on speaking terms. It means your children may be temporarily sad, but they feel secure and loved. And, crucially, it means you resisted falling into the traps that the system sets up along the way: a discouragement of off-the-record discourse between spouses, a hyper-willingness to go for the jugular, an us-versus-them mentality, and an expensive make-work process of letter writing and motion filing that will bring your bank account to its knees.

Too many attorneys drive their clients to a process that fits *the attorney's needs* and not necessarily what works best for families. Now that your blinders are off, however, you can avoid the pitfalls discussed in this book. You can take charge of your divorce and make your lawyer work for you, rather than being a passive participant in this process.

So you're in charge. Now what? As you take the reins of your divorce, one challenge you may face is to maintain a rational thought process relating to your case when feelings of sadness, anger, and resentment can seem overwhelming. Though this will certainly involve some mental jiu-jitsu, separating the negotiation element of divorce from your emotional experience is a key step in achieving a positive result. Conversely, working out your emotional issues within the context of your divorce often leads you down a path of unreasonable demands, irreparable damage to relationships, unhappy outcomes, and huge legal fees. Your lawyer is not your therapist. This is where your self-awareness will come into play. Be cognizant of how your underlying emotions may be whispering in your ear, undermining the more reasonable voices of compromise and sanity. (*i.e.*"Why should I give him that holiday weekend with our kid? He was never there for us before." Or, "She must never have loved me at all if she's asking for this much. I'm putting my foot down.") Listen for your own crazy thoughts (you *will* have them), and resist them as you work towards your settlement. It may be helpful to seek out a counselor as you work through these tough emotions. Seeking temporary professional help is a far preferable option than leaning on your (expensive and untrained) lawyer for emotional support.

As you keep a firm hold on your emotions, you may have some slip-ups along the way: moments of anger and impatience and unreasonableness, and so will your spouse. Divorce is an utterly human process that can shine a bright, unforgiving light on our worst selves. Be patient with yourself and with your spouse when these challenging moments occur.

Men and women tend to approach this process very differently, exacerbating the potential for misunderstanding and blame. Once a man gets over the initial emotional hurdle of divorce, he will likely be very outcome-focused: let's get this done, I've made a list of XYZ, here's the account information. He's taken a tough, painful swallow of hurt, and now it's time to move on. But while a man tends to think in terms of unemotional resolutions at this point, a woman may still be processing. In my experience, women need more time to ruminate over the emotional elements of divorce. Time and again, I've seen a man raring to go, to get on with it, while his spouse lags behind. To him, it seems as if she's deliberately delaying proceedings. Frustrated by her seemingly lackadaisical approach, he feels impatient and manipulated. From her perspective, she feels rushed and off-balance.

The solution to this dynamic is two-fold. First, even if you don't want to, you have to communicate about your divorce. This is so difficult because usually one or both of the parties must deal with feelings of rejection. If you need more time, say so. There's nothing wrong with needing more time to evaluate and process so you can move forward in the best way possible.

Second, although it may be human nature to create entire stories about the other person's motivations, it's most often the case that they're simply doing the best that they can. Resist jumping to ugly conclusions regarding your spouse's approach to your divorce. After all, this is one of life's extreme moments – go easy on one another. Signing a divorce truce, as we discussed in Chapter 4, can be a good way to keep your hearts – and the lines of communication – open.

The Final Takeaway

When all is said and done, divorce provides you with a choice. You can come out the other side of it depleted and resentful or you can emerge a better person and a better parent. At the risk of sounding crazy, ask yourself: How is this the best thing that's ever happened to me? I have handled enough of these case to tell you that your divorce can make you a wiser, stronger, better person. And while this can seem like your darkest days, I promise there are new opportunities on the horizon now that you're beginning a new chapter in your life.

Some transitions in life are more traumatic than others; for most people, divorce is a wrenching shock to the system. But with this jolt comes a gift, should you choose to accept it. It can force upon you a moment of clarity and an opportunity for rebirth that you wouldn't receive any other way. It is my hope that you achieve a good divorce so that you can eventually get to great.

Recap of Free Information Offered Earlier In This Book

Divorce Truce Document

If you would like a free copy of the Divorce Truce agreement that I encourage my clients and their spouse to use at the very beginning please enter the following website address into the URL address line of your favorite Browser (be sure to use lower case letters):

www. 24HourDivorceLawyer.com/truce

"Picking the Right Divorce" Cheat Sheet
www. 24HourDivorceLawyer.com/cheatsheet

Free Divorce Tools
Modifiable Budget:
www. 24HourDivorceLawyer.com/budget

Modifiable asset and liability worksheet:
www. 24HourDivorceLawyer.com/worksheet

If Your Case Is In New Mexico, Colorado or Nebraska, We Can Help.

Please visit us at one of our Websites below or call our office for an appointment.

For Cases in New Mexico

www.NewMexicoLegalGroup.com

For Cases in Colorado

www.ColoradoLegalGroup.com

For Cases in Nebraska

www.NebraskaLegalGroup.com

Made in the USA
San Bernardino, CA
04 June 2020

72724205R00115